HOW TO START A DELIVERY BUSINESS

Introduction

Welcome to the comprehensive guide on starting and scaling a successful delivery business! Whether you're venturing into the logistics industry for the first time or seeking to expand your existing operations, this book is designed to equip you with the knowledge, strategies, and insights needed to navigate the complexities of the delivery business landscape.

In these pages, you'll discover practical advice, actionable steps, and expert tips gathered from industry leaders and successful entrepreneurs. From understanding the fundamentals of logistics and operational management to harnessing the power of technology and innovation, each chapter is crafted to empower you in building a resilient and thriving delivery enterprise.

Whether your goal is to optimize delivery routes, enhance customer experience, embrace sustainable practices, or explore emerging trends like autonomous vehicles and drone deliveries, this book will serve as your trusted companion. Together, we'll explore every aspect of running a delivery business with a focus on efficiency, customer satisfaction, and sustainable growth.

Get ready to embark on a journey of learning, inspiration, and transformation. Let's dive in and pave the way for your delivery business success!

Copyright © 2024

All rights reserved. No part of this book may be reproduced in any form or by any electronic or mechanical means, including information storage and retrieval systems, without permission in writing from the publisher, except by a reviewer, who may quote brief passages in a review.

The information contained in this book is for general information purposes only. The information is provided by naciro and while we endeavor to keep the information up to date and correct, we make no representations or warranties of any kind, express or implied, about the completeness, accuracy, reliability, suitability or availability with respect to the book or the information, products, services, or related graphics contained in the book for any purpose. Any reliance you place on such information is therefore strictly at your own risk.

All trademarks and registered trademarks are the property of their respective owners and are used in this book only for identification and explanation.

Permission to use copyrighted material in this book should be obtained from the copyright owner or the publisher.

This book is not intended to provide medical, legal, or financial advice, and the author and publisher specifically disclaim any liability for any loss or damage caused or alleged to be caused directly or indirectly by the information in this book.

Naciro and the publisher of this book do not endorse or recommend any commercial products, processes, or services. The views and opinions of authors expressed in this book do not necessarily state or reflect those of the publisher of this book.

Contents

Chapter 1: Introduction to Starting Your Delivery Business

Chapter 2: Understanding the Market Demand for Your Delivery Business

Chapter 3: Researching Your Target Audience and Niche Market

Chapter 4: Analyzing Competitors in the Delivery Industry

Chapter 5: Legal and Regulatory Considerations for Starting a Delivery Business

Chapter 6: Creating a Comprehensive Business Plan for Your Delivery Business

Chapter 7: Setting Up Your Delivery Operations

Chapter 8: Effective Marketing Strategies for Your Delivery Business

Chapter 9: Financial Management Strategies for Your Delivery Business

Chapter 10: Operational Efficiency Strategies for Your Delivery Business

Chapter 11: Scaling and Expanding Your Delivery Business

Chapter 12: Embracing Sustainability in Your Delivery Business

Chapter 13: Future Trends and Innovations in the Delivery Industry

Chapter 14: Workforce Management and Employee Engagement in Your Delivery Business

Chapter 15: Customer Retention Strategies and Building Loyalty in Your Delivery Business

Chapter 16: Crisis Management Strategies for Your Delivery Business

Chapter 17: Emerging Technologies in the Delivery Industry

Chapter 18: Strategic Marketing for Your Delivery Business

Chapter 19: Financial Management for Your Delivery Business

Chapter 20: Legal Considerations for Your Delivery Business

Chapter 21: Customer Service Excellence in Your Delivery Business

Chapter 22: Managing and Optimizing Your Delivery Fleet

Chapter 23: Marketing Strategies for Your Delivery Business

Chapter 24: Customer Retention Strategies for Your Delivery Business

Chapter 25: Advanced Financial Management for Your Delivery Business

Chapter 26: Embracing Technological Innovations in the Delivery Industry

Chapter 27: Scaling Your Delivery Business for Growth

Chapter 28: Enhancing Customer Experience in Your Delivery Business

Chapter 29: The Future of Delivery Logistics: Emerging Trends and Technologies

Chapter 1: Introduction to Starting Your Delivery Business

Welcome to the exciting journey of starting your own delivery business! Whether you're passionate about logistics, eager to capitalize on the booming e-commerce industry, or simply looking to fill a niche in your community, starting a delivery service opens up a world of opportunities.

Why Start a Delivery Business?

Imagine a world where people can have almost anything they want delivered right to their doorstep with just a few taps on their smartphones. This convenience-driven era has transformed how goods are bought and sold, creating a robust demand for efficient delivery services. From groceries and restaurant meals to electronics and healthcare supplies, the need for reliable, timely delivery solutions is greater than ever before.

Understanding the Market Landscape

Before diving headfirst into your business venture, it's crucial to understand the market landscape. Take time to research current trends in delivery services. Who are your potential customers? What types of products or services are in high demand for delivery? Are there gaps in the market that your business can fill?

E-commerce giants have set high standards for fast, reliable deliveries, setting consumer expectations at an all-time high. However, there's also room for local, specialized delivery services that offer personalized, community-focused experiences. By identifying your target market and understanding their needs, you can position your delivery business strategically for success.

The Benefits of Starting Small

Starting small doesn't mean thinking small. In fact, many successful delivery businesses began with humble beginnings, serving a specific neighborhood or niche market. By focusing on a smaller area or specific service category initially, you can refine your operations, build a loyal customer base, and perfect your service offerings before scaling up.

Passion and Commitment: Key Ingredients for Success

Passion fuels commitment, and commitment fuels success. Starting and running a delivery business requires dedication, perseverance, and a genuine passion for delivering exceptional service. Your enthusiasm will drive you through the challenges and uncertainties that come with entrepreneurship.

Embracing Innovation and Technology

Technology has revolutionized the delivery industry, offering tools and platforms that streamline operations and enhance customer experiences. From route optimization software and GPS tracking systems to mobile apps and online ordering platforms, embracing innovative technologies can give your business a competitive edge.

Building Strong Relationships

Relationships are at the heart of any successful business. Whether it's forging partnerships with local businesses, nurturing relationships with suppliers, or providing outstanding customer service, building strong relationships is key to long-term success. People are more likely to trust and support businesses that prioritize relationships and community involvement.

Your Business Plan: Blueprint for Success

A well-crafted business plan serves as your roadmap, outlining your business goals, target market, competitive analysis, marketing strategy, financial projections, and more. It's not just a document for investors; it's a tool to guide your decisions and measure your progress as you grow your delivery business.

Overcoming Challenges

Every business faces challenges, and the delivery industry is no exception. From logistical hurdles and unpredictable weather to fierce competition and customer expectations, being prepared to adapt and innovate is crucial. By anticipating challenges and having contingency plans in place, you can navigate obstacles with confidence.

The Reward of Making a Difference

Beyond profits and growth, starting a delivery business allows you to make a tangible difference in people's lives. Whether you're providing essential goods to those who can't easily access them or helping local businesses thrive by reaching a broader audience, the impact of your service extends far beyond delivery.

Conclusion

Starting a delivery business is a rewarding journey filled with opportunities to innovate, connect with your community, and make a positive impact. As you embark on this adventure, remember to stay curious, stay passionate, and stay committed to delivering excellence every step of the way.

Chapter 2: Understanding the Market Demand for Your Delivery Business

Welcome to Chapter 2 of your journey into starting a delivery business! In this chapter, we'll delve into understanding the market demand—a critical foundation for the success of your venture.

Why Market Demand Matters

Before you start any business, it's essential to assess whether there is a viable market demand for your services. In the case of a delivery business, this involves understanding who your potential customers are, what they need delivered, and how often they need it. By identifying and addressing these factors, you can position your business to meet real market needs effectively.

Identifying Your Target Audience

One of the first steps in understanding market demand is identifying your target audience. Consider demographics such as age, location, income level, and lifestyle habits. Are you targeting busy professionals who need meal deliveries? Or perhaps elderly individuals who require prescription medication deliveries? By defining your target audience, you can tailor your services and marketing strategies to appeal directly to their needs and preferences.

Researching Market Trends and Opportunities

Market trends play a significant role in shaping the demand for delivery services. Stay informed about current trends in consumer behavior, such as the rise of online shopping, the demand for fast and convenient deliveries, and the preference for eco-friendly packaging options. Additionally, keep an eye on emerging opportunities, such as niche markets or underserved areas where your delivery business could fill a gap.

Analyzing Competitor Landscape

Competitor analysis is another crucial aspect of understanding market demand. Research existing delivery businesses in your area or within your niche. What services do they offer? How do they price their deliveries? What are their strengths and weaknesses? By conducting a thorough competitor analysis, you can identify opportunities for differentiation and innovation to stand out in the competitive landscape.

Conducting Market Research

Market research involves gathering and analyzing data to gain insights into customer preferences, purchasing behavior, and market dynamics. Techniques such as surveys, focus groups, and interviews with potential customers can provide valuable feedback and validate your business idea. Use this information to refine your service offerings, pricing strategy, and marketing approach based on real customer insights.

Assessing Seasonal and Cyclical Demand

Consider how seasonal and cyclical factors may impact demand for your delivery services. For example, certain industries may experience peak seasons (e.g., holidays, back-to-school periods) where demand for deliveries spikes. Understanding these patterns allows you to anticipate fluctuations in demand and adjust your operations accordingly, such as staffing levels and inventory management.

Addressing Evolving Customer Expectations

In today's competitive marketplace, customer expectations for delivery services are constantly evolving. Consumers expect transparency, reliability, and convenience throughout the delivery process. Consider offering options such as real-time tracking, flexible delivery windows, and hassle-free returns to enhance the customer experience. By meeting and exceeding these expectations, you can build customer loyalty and differentiate your business from competitors.

Leveraging Technology for Competitive Advantage

Technology plays a pivotal role in meeting market demand effectively. Invest in delivery management software, GPS tracking systems, and mobile apps to streamline operations, optimize routes, and enhance communication with customers. Embracing technology not only improves efficiency but also allows you to deliver a seamless and satisfying experience that keeps customers coming back.

Conclusion

Understanding market demand is the cornerstone of a successful delivery business. By identifying your target audience, researching market trends, analyzing competitors, conducting thorough market research, and leveraging technology, you can position your business to meet and exceed customer expectations. Stay adaptable and responsive to changes in consumer behavior and market dynamics to sustain long-term growth and profitability.

In the next chapter, we'll explore how to research your target audience and niche market in greater detail, helping you refine your business strategy and set the stage for a successful launch. Get ready to dive deeper into the specifics of who you'll be serving and how you can meet their delivery needs with excellence.

Chapter 3: Researching Your Target Audience and Niche Market

Welcome to Chapter 3 of your journey into starting a delivery business! In this chapter, we'll explore the importance of researching your target audience and niche market—a critical step in shaping your business strategy and ensuring long-term success.

Why Research Your Target Audience?

Understanding your target audience goes beyond demographics; it's about gaining deep insights into their needs, preferences, and behaviors. By identifying who your potential customers are and what motivates their purchasing decisions, you can tailor your delivery services to meet their specific expectations effectively.

Defining Your Target Audience

Start by defining the demographics of your target audience, such as age, gender, income level, and location. Consider psychographic factors as well, including lifestyle preferences, values, and buying habits. For example, are you targeting busy professionals who value convenience, or health-conscious individuals seeking organic food deliveries? By creating detailed customer personas, you can visualize and empathize with your target audience, allowing you to craft personalized marketing messages and service offerings that resonate with them.

Conducting Market Segmentation

Market segmentation involves dividing your target audience into distinct groups based on shared characteristics or needs. This allows you to prioritize segments with the highest potential for profitability and tailor your marketing efforts accordingly. Segment your audience based on factors such as geographic location, purchasing behavior, and product preferences to identify niche markets or underserved segments where your delivery business can thrive.

Analyzing Customer Needs and Pain Points

Researching your target audience involves understanding their needs, desires, and pain points related to delivery services. What challenges do they currently face with existing delivery options? Are there specific features or benefits they prioritize when choosing a delivery service? By conducting surveys, interviews, or focus groups with potential customers, you can gather valuable feedback that informs your service offerings and helps you address customer pain points effectively.

Studying Consumer Behavior and Trends

Consumer behavior is influenced by various factors, including economic conditions, cultural trends, and technological advancements. Stay informed about current trends in consumer preferences for delivery services, such as the demand for eco-friendly packaging, preference for contactless delivery options, or interest in subscription-based delivery models. By aligning your business with these trends, you can anticipate market shifts and position your delivery services as relevant and appealing to your target audience.

Assessing Competitive Landscape

Analyze the competitive landscape within your niche market to identify strengths, weaknesses, and opportunities for differentiation. Research existing delivery businesses that cater to similar customer segments or offer similar services. What unique value propositions do they offer? How can you differentiate your delivery business through superior service, innovative solutions, or personalized customer experiences? Understanding your competitors' strategies allows you to refine your own business approach and identify gaps in the market that your delivery business can fill.

Leveraging Digital Tools and Analytics

Utilize digital tools and analytics to gather actionable insights about your target audience and market performance. Implement customer relationship management (CRM) software to track customer interactions and preferences. Use website analytics and social media insights to monitor engagement metrics and understand how customers interact with your brand online. By leveraging data-driven insights, you can make informed decisions that optimize your marketing campaigns, improve customer retention, and drive business growth.

Conclusion

Researching your target audience and niche market is a foundational step in building a successful delivery business. By defining your target audience, conducting market segmentation, analyzing customer needs and behaviors, studying market trends, assessing the competitive landscape, and leveraging digital tools, you can gain a deep understanding of your market dynamics and position your delivery business for sustainable growth and profitability.

In the next chapter, we'll delve into conducting competitive analysis and understanding your competitors' strengths and weaknesses. This will equip you with valuable insights to differentiate your delivery business and capture market opportunities effectively. Get ready to refine your business strategy and set yourself apart in the competitive landscape of delivery services.

Chapter 4: Analyzing Competitors in the Delivery Industry

Welcome to Chapter 4 of your journey into starting a delivery business! In this chapter, we'll explore the importance of analyzing competitors in the delivery industry and how it can guide your business strategy for success.

Understanding the Competitive Landscape

Analyzing your competitors is not about copying their strategies but rather understanding their strengths, weaknesses, and market positioning. By gaining insights into what your competitors are doing well and where they fall short, you can identify opportunities to differentiate your delivery business and carve out a unique space in the market.

Types of Competitors to Consider

Competitors in the delivery industry can vary widely, from large multinational logistics companies to local courier services and innovative startups. Consider both direct competitors—those offering similar delivery services or targeting the same customer segments—and indirect competitors—businesses offering alternative solutions that fulfill similar customer needs.

Conducting Competitive Analysis

1. **Identify Competitors**: Start by identifying key competitors within your geographic area or niche market. Use online research, industry publications, and local business directories to compile a list of competitors.
2. **Evaluate Services Offered**: Analyze the range of services offered by your competitors. What types of deliveries do they specialize in? Do they offer same-day delivery, specialized packaging, or additional services such as assembly or installation?
3. **Assess Pricing Strategies**: Evaluate how competitors price their delivery services. Are they competitive on price, or do they

differentiate based on premium services or added value? Consider how your pricing strategy can attract price-sensitive customers or justify premium pricing with superior service.
4. **Study Customer Reviews and Feedback**: Review customer feedback and online reviews to understand how customers perceive your competitors' services. What do customers appreciate about their experiences, and where do they express dissatisfaction? Use this feedback to identify areas where you can excel and exceed customer expectations.
5. **Analyze Marketing and Branding**: Examine competitors' marketing strategies, branding efforts, and online presence. How do they position themselves in the market? Are there opportunities to differentiate your brand through innovative marketing campaigns, unique value propositions, or targeted messaging that resonates with your target audience?
6. **Evaluate Operational Efficiency**: Assess competitors' operational efficiency, including delivery times, reliability, and customer service responsiveness. Identify potential gaps in service quality or operational inefficiencies that you can address to offer a superior customer experience.

Differentiating Your Delivery Business

Based on your competitive analysis, identify opportunities to differentiate your delivery business and create a competitive advantage:

- **Unique Value Proposition**: Develop a clear and compelling value proposition that highlights what sets your delivery services apart from competitors. Whether it's exceptional customer service, innovative technology solutions, or specialized delivery capabilities, articulate why customers should choose your business over alternatives.
- **Focus on Niche Markets**: Consider specializing in niche markets or underserved customer segments where competitors may not be fully addressing customer needs. Tailor your services to meet specific industry requirements or demographic preferences to

attract loyal customers who value your expertise and specialization.
- **Innovative Solutions**: Innovate by introducing new delivery technologies, eco-friendly practices, or value-added services that differentiate your business and enhance customer satisfaction. Embrace opportunities for continuous improvement and stay ahead of evolving customer expectations and industry trends.

Conclusion

Analyzing competitors in the delivery industry provides valuable insights that inform strategic decision-making and position your business for success. By understanding competitors' strengths, weaknesses, and market strategies, you can identify opportunities to differentiate your delivery business, attract customers, and achieve sustainable growth.

In the next chapter, we'll explore the legal and regulatory considerations for starting a delivery business. Understanding the legal landscape and compliance requirements is essential for operating your business responsibly and mitigating risks. Get ready to navigate the regulatory framework and set a solid foundation for your delivery business journey.

Chapter 5: Legal and Regulatory Considerations for Starting a Delivery Business

Welcome to Chapter 5 of your journey into starting a delivery business! In this chapter, we'll navigate through the essential legal and regulatory considerations you need to understand and comply with to launch and operate your delivery business successfully.

Importance of Legal Compliance

Navigating the legal landscape is crucial for any business, and the delivery industry is no exception. Compliance with laws and regulations not only ensures the legality of your operations but also protects your business from potential fines, penalties, and legal disputes. By understanding and adhering to legal requirements, you can build a foundation for sustainable growth and mitigate risks.

Choosing Your Business Structure

One of the first decisions you'll need to make is choosing the right legal structure for your delivery business. Common options include:

- **Sole Proprietorship**: Simplest form of business structure where you are personally liable for business debts.
- **Partnership**: Formed with one or more partners sharing ownership and liability.
- **Limited Liability Company (LLC)**: Provides personal liability protection while offering flexibility in management and tax treatment.
- **Corporation**: Offers the highest level of personal liability protection but involves more formalities and taxation considerations.

Consult with a legal advisor or business attorney to determine the most suitable structure based on your business goals, risk tolerance, and tax implications.

Registering Your Business

Once you've chosen a business structure, you'll need to register your delivery business with the appropriate government authorities. This typically involves registering your business name, obtaining an employer identification number (EIN) from the IRS for tax purposes, and complying with local business licensing requirements. Check with your state and local government offices or online resources to ensure you meet all registration and licensing obligations.

Obtaining Permits and Licenses

Depending on the nature of your delivery services and location, you may need specific permits and licenses to legally operate your business. Common permits and licenses for delivery businesses may include:

- **Business License**: Required for operating a business within a specific jurisdiction.
- **Transportation Permits**: Depending on the type of deliveries (e.g., food, hazardous materials), you may need special permits from local or state authorities.
- **Vehicle Registration and Insurance**: Ensure your delivery vehicles are properly registered and insured according to local regulations.

Research and comply with all applicable federal, state, and local regulations to avoid penalties and ensure smooth operations.

Understanding Employment Laws

If you plan to hire delivery personnel or staff for your operations, familiarize yourself with employment laws and regulations. This includes:

- **Wage and Hour Laws**: Ensure compliance with minimum wage requirements and overtime pay regulations.

- **Worker Classification**: Understand the distinction between employees and independent contractors, as misclassification can lead to legal liabilities.
- **Safety Regulations**: Provide a safe working environment and comply with Occupational Safety and Health Administration (OSHA) standards.

Consult with a legal advisor or employment law specialist to navigate these regulations and protect both your business and employees.

Compliance with Delivery Regulations

Certain industries, such as pharmaceuticals or food delivery, may have specific regulations governing the handling and transportation of goods. Ensure compliance with industry-specific regulations, including:

- **Food Safety and Handling**: If offering food delivery services, adhere to local health department regulations for food safety and sanitation.
- **Healthcare Delivery**: Comply with regulations for transporting medical supplies and pharmaceuticals, including proper storage and handling practices.

Data Privacy and Security

In today's digital age, protecting customer data is paramount. Implement policies and procedures to safeguard sensitive information collected during order processing and delivery operations. Familiarize yourself with data privacy laws, such as the General Data Protection Regulation (GDPR) if applicable, and ensure compliance with customer consent requirements for data collection and use.

Insurance Coverage

Protect your business and assets with adequate insurance coverage tailored to the risks associated with delivery operations. Consider obtaining:

- **General Liability Insurance**: Coverage for bodily injury, property damage, and personal injury claims.
- **Commercial Auto Insurance**: Insurance for vehicles used in business operations, including delivery vehicles.
- **Cargo Insurance**: Coverage for goods in transit against loss or damage during delivery.

Review your insurance needs with an insurance agent familiar with the delivery industry to ensure comprehensive coverage.

Conclusion

Navigating the legal and regulatory landscape may seem daunting, but it's essential for the long-term success and sustainability of your delivery business. By understanding and complying with legal requirements, choosing the right business structure, obtaining necessary permits and licenses, adhering to employment laws, and protecting customer data, you can establish a solid legal foundation for your business.

In the next chapter, we'll dive deeper into creating a comprehensive business plan for your delivery business. A well-crafted business plan serves as a roadmap for success, outlining your goals, strategies, financial projections, and operational framework. Get ready to outline your path to achieving your business aspirations and delivering excellence to your customers.

Chapter 6: Creating a Comprehensive Business Plan for Your Delivery Business

Welcome to Chapter 6 of your journey into starting a delivery business! In this chapter, we'll explore the essential steps and components of creating a comprehensive business plan that will guide your business towards success.

Importance of a Business Plan

A business plan serves as a roadmap for your delivery business, outlining your goals, strategies, financial projections, and operational framework. It's not just a document for investors; it's a tool that helps you clarify your vision, make informed decisions, and navigate challenges effectively. Whether you're seeking financing or starting small, a well-crafted business plan sets the foundation for sustainable growth and profitability.

Executive Summary

The executive summary provides a concise overview of your delivery business plan, highlighting key aspects such as your business concept, target market, competitive advantage, and financial projections. While it appears first in your business plan, it's often written last as a summary of the entire document.

Business Description and Vision

Describe your delivery business in detail, including the products or services you will offer, your unique value proposition, and your mission statement. Articulate your vision for the business—what do you hope to achieve, and how do you envision your business evolving over time?

Market Analysis

Conduct a thorough analysis of the market for delivery services, including trends, customer demographics, competitive landscape, and growth potential. Identify your target audience and niche markets, and explain how your delivery business will meet their needs better than competitors.

Organization and Management Structure

Outline the organizational structure of your delivery business, including key roles and responsibilities. Describe the management team's experience and qualifications, highlighting any relevant industry expertise or entrepreneurial achievements. Investors and stakeholders want to know that your team has the skills and knowledge to execute your business plan effectively.

Product or Service Offering

Detail the specific products or services your delivery business will offer. Are you specializing in same-day deliveries, subscription services, or specialized delivery solutions for certain industries? Explain the features and benefits of your offerings and how they address customer pain points or fulfill market demand.

Marketing and Sales Strategy

Develop a comprehensive marketing and sales strategy to attract and retain customers. Identify your target audience and outline your promotional tactics, including digital marketing, social media campaigns, partnerships with local businesses, and community outreach initiatives. Define your pricing strategy and sales projections based on market research and competitive analysis.

Operational Plan

Describe the operational aspects of your delivery business, including logistics, fleet management, and customer service. Detail your delivery process—from order placement and fulfillment to delivery tracking and customer support. Address scalability and operational efficiencies, outlining how you will manage growth while maintaining service quality and customer satisfaction.

Financial Projections

Create detailed financial projections for your delivery business, including income statements, cash flow forecasts, and break-even analysis. Estimate startup costs, ongoing expenses, and revenue projections based on market demand and pricing strategy. Investors and lenders will evaluate your financial projections to assess the feasibility and potential profitability of your business.

Funding Requirements

If seeking financing or investment, specify your funding requirements in your business plan. Outline how much capital you need to launch and grow your delivery business, how you plan to use the funds, and the expected return on investment for stakeholders. Detail any existing capital, loans, or personal investment in the business.

Risk Analysis and Contingency Planning

Identify potential risks and challenges that may impact your delivery business, such as market competition, regulatory changes, or operational disruptions. Develop contingency plans and risk mitigation strategies to address these challenges proactively. Investors and stakeholders will appreciate your preparedness and foresight in managing potential risks.

Conclusion

Creating a comprehensive business plan for your delivery business is a crucial step towards achieving your entrepreneurial goals. By outlining your business concept, market analysis, organizational structure, marketing strategy, operational plan, financial projections, and risk management strategies, you can demonstrate your readiness to launch and grow a successful delivery business.

In the next chapter, we'll explore the practical aspects of setting up your delivery operations, including logistics management, technology integration, and customer service excellence. Get ready to turn your business plan into action and start delivering exceptional service to your customers.

Chapter 7: Setting Up Your Delivery Operations

Welcome to Chapter 7 of your journey into starting a delivery business! In this chapter, we'll delve into the practical aspects of setting up your delivery operations—from logistics management and technology integration to ensuring exceptional customer service.

Establishing Logistics Management

Logistics management is at the core of your delivery operations, encompassing everything from inventory management to route optimization and last-mile delivery. Consider the following steps to establish efficient logistics:

1. **Inventory Management**: Implement inventory systems to track stock levels, manage orders, and ensure timely replenishment of goods. This helps prevent stockouts and improves order fulfillment efficiency.
2. **Warehouse Organization**: Organize your warehouse or storage facility to facilitate easy access and efficient picking and packing of orders. Utilize shelving, labeling systems, and inventory categorization for streamlined operations.
3. **Routing and Scheduling**: Use route optimization software to plan delivery routes based on factors like distance, traffic patterns, and delivery time windows. Efficient routing reduces fuel costs, minimizes delivery times, and enhances overall customer satisfaction.
4. **Fleet Management**: Maintain your delivery vehicles regularly to ensure reliability and minimize downtime. Implement vehicle tracking systems for real-time monitoring of fleet operations, including driver location and delivery status updates.

Integrating Technology Solutions

Technology plays a crucial role in optimizing delivery operations and enhancing customer experiences. Consider integrating the following technology solutions:

1. **Delivery Management Software**: Use specialized software to automate order processing, track deliveries in real-time, and manage customer communications. These tools streamline operations and improve efficiency.
2. **GPS Tracking Systems**: Equip delivery vehicles with GPS tracking devices to monitor routes, driver behavior, and delivery progress. Real-time tracking enhances transparency and allows customers to track their orders.
3. **Mobile Applications**: Develop a user-friendly mobile app for customers to place orders, track deliveries, and provide feedback. An intuitive app improves convenience and engagement, fostering customer loyalty.
4. **Digital Payments**: Offer secure digital payment options to streamline transactions and enhance customer convenience. Accepting online payments reduces administrative tasks and accelerates order processing.

Ensuring Exceptional Customer Service

Customer service is a cornerstone of successful delivery operations. Here's how to ensure exceptional service:

1. **Clear Communication**: Provide clear and timely communication with customers regarding order status, delivery updates, and any issues that may arise. Proactive communication builds trust and reduces customer anxiety.
2. **Responsive Support**: Establish a dedicated customer support team to address inquiries, resolve issues promptly, and provide assistance throughout the delivery process. Offer multiple communication channels, such as phone, email, and live chat, for accessibility.
3. **Delivery Experience**: Focus on delivering a positive experience from start to finish. Train delivery personnel to handle packages with care, adhere to delivery instructions, and provide courteous service at customers' doorsteps.
4. **Feedback Collection**: Solicit feedback from customers to gauge satisfaction levels and identify areas for improvement. Use

customer feedback to refine your services, address common issues, and enhance overall service quality.

Implementing Sustainability Practices

As sustainability becomes increasingly important to consumers, consider implementing eco-friendly practices in your delivery operations:

1. **Optimized Routes**: Efficient route planning reduces fuel consumption and minimizes carbon emissions. Choose eco-friendly delivery vehicles or explore options for electric or hybrid vehicles to lower your environmental footprint.
2. **Packaging Solutions**: Use recyclable or biodegradable packaging materials to reduce waste. Encourage customers to opt for minimal packaging or reusable containers where possible.
3. **Carbon Offsetting**: Offset carbon emissions from delivery operations by participating in carbon offset programs or investing in renewable energy initiatives. Communicate your commitment to sustainability to resonate with environmentally conscious customers.

Conclusion

Setting up your delivery operations requires careful planning, integration of technology solutions, and a commitment to exceptional customer service. By establishing efficient logistics management, integrating technology for optimization, ensuring exceptional customer experiences, and implementing sustainability practices, you can build a foundation for success in the competitive delivery industry.

In the next chapter, we'll explore effective marketing strategies to promote your delivery business and attract customers. From digital marketing tactics to community engagement initiatives, get ready to elevate your brand presence and drive growth in your target market.

Chapter 8: Effective Marketing Strategies for Your Delivery Business

Welcome to Chapter 8 of your journey into starting a delivery business! In this chapter, we'll explore effective marketing strategies to promote your delivery services, attract customers, and build a strong brand presence in your target market.

Understanding Your Target Audience

Before diving into marketing tactics, it's crucial to understand your target audience—the individuals or businesses most likely to use your delivery services. Consider demographics, psychographics, and behaviors that influence their purchasing decisions. Are you targeting busy professionals, health-conscious consumers, or businesses needing logistical support? Understanding your audience enables you to tailor your marketing efforts for maximum impact.

Developing Your Brand Identity

Your brand identity is more than just a logo; it's the essence of your delivery business. Develop a compelling brand story that resonates with your target audience. Define your brand values, mission, and unique value proposition (UVP)—what sets your delivery services apart from competitors? Consistent branding across all channels builds trust and recognition among customers.

Building a Professional Website

In today's digital age, a professional website serves as your online storefront. Create a user-friendly website that showcases your delivery services, pricing options, and customer testimonials. Include an easy-to-navigate interface for placing orders and accessing customer support. Optimize your website for search engines (SEO) to improve visibility and attract organic traffic from potential customers searching for delivery services online.

Leveraging Social Media Marketing

Social media platforms are powerful tools for connecting with your audience and promoting your delivery business. Establish a presence on platforms relevant to your target audience, such as Facebook, Instagram, LinkedIn, or Twitter. Share engaging content, such as delivery tips, behind-the-scenes stories, customer testimonials, and promotional offers. Use targeted advertising to reach specific demographics and encourage interaction through comments, likes, and shares to increase brand awareness.

Implementing Content Marketing Strategies

Content marketing involves creating valuable, relevant content to attract and engage your target audience. Develop blog posts, articles, infographics, or videos that address common delivery challenges, industry trends, or customer interests. Position your delivery business as a thought leader by sharing expertise and providing solutions to audience pain points. Distribute content through your website, social media channels, email newsletters, and industry publications to establish credibility and drive traffic to your business.

Utilizing Email Marketing Campaigns

Email marketing remains an effective way to nurture relationships with current and potential customers. Build an email list through website sign-ups, order confirmations, or promotional offers. Segment your email list based on customer preferences or purchase history to personalize content and promotions. Send targeted campaigns, such as new service announcements, special discounts, or seasonal promotions, to encourage repeat business and keep your delivery services top-of-mind.

Partnering with Local Businesses

Form strategic partnerships with local businesses to expand your customer base and enhance brand visibility. Collaborate with restaurants, retailers, or e-commerce platforms that require reliable delivery services. Offer exclusive discounts or bundled services to incentivize partnerships. Participate in community events, sponsorships, or charity initiatives to demonstrate your commitment to local engagement and build trust within your community.

Monitoring and Analyzing Marketing Performance

Track key performance indicators (KPIs) to measure the effectiveness of your marketing strategies and adjust tactics accordingly. Monitor metrics such as website traffic, social media engagement, conversion rates, and customer acquisition costs. Use analytics tools to gain insights into customer behavior, campaign effectiveness, and ROI. Continuously optimize your marketing efforts based on data-driven insights to maximize results and achieve your business goals.

Seeking Customer Feedback and Reviews

Encourage satisfied customers to leave reviews and testimonials about their experiences with your delivery services. Positive reviews build credibility and influence potential customers' purchasing decisions. Respond promptly to customer feedback, whether positive or negative, to demonstrate responsiveness and commitment to customer satisfaction. Use feedback to identify areas for improvement and refine your service offerings to meet customer expectations consistently.

Conclusion

Effective marketing strategies are essential for promoting your delivery business, attracting customers, and establishing a strong brand presence in the competitive marketplace. By understanding your target audience, developing a compelling brand identity, leveraging digital marketing channels, and analyzing performance metrics, you can create impactful campaigns that drive awareness, engagement, and growth for your delivery business.

In the next chapter, we'll explore financial management strategies for your delivery business. From budgeting and pricing strategies to managing cash flow and forecasting expenses, get ready to navigate the financial aspects of running a successful delivery operation.

Chapter 9: Financial Management Strategies for Your Delivery Business

Welcome to Chapter 9 of your journey into starting a delivery business! In this chapter, we'll explore essential financial management strategies to help you effectively manage finances, maximize profitability, and ensure the long-term financial health of your delivery business.

Budgeting for Your Delivery Business

Budgeting is a fundamental aspect of financial management, providing a roadmap for allocating resources and managing expenses. Start by creating a detailed budget that encompasses both startup costs and ongoing operational expenses. Consider the following components:

1. **Startup Costs**: Identify initial expenses such as vehicle purchase or lease, equipment (e.g., GPS systems, packaging materials), insurance premiums, legal fees, and marketing launch campaigns.
2. **Operational Expenses**: Estimate recurring costs such as vehicle maintenance, fuel or electricity for vehicles, warehouse rent, utilities, payroll (if hiring staff), marketing and advertising, software subscriptions, and insurance renewals.
3. **Contingency Fund**: Set aside a contingency fund for unexpected expenses or fluctuations in revenue. Aim to maintain a buffer to cover at least three to six months of operating expenses to mitigate financial risks.

Pricing Strategies for Delivery Services

Developing a competitive pricing strategy is essential for profitability while remaining attractive to customers. Consider factors such as:

1. **Cost Structure**: Calculate all costs associated with delivery operations, including vehicle maintenance, fuel, labor, insurance, and overhead expenses.

2. **Market Analysis**: Research competitors' pricing models and customer expectations in your target market. Determine whether you will offer competitive pricing, premium pricing for added value services, or a cost-leadership approach to capture market share.
3. **Value-Based Pricing**: Consider pricing based on the value delivered to customers, such as speed of delivery, reliability, and additional services offered. Communicate the benefits of your pricing structure to justify costs to customers.

Managing Cash Flow Effectively

Cash flow management is crucial for maintaining liquidity and sustaining day-to-day operations. Implement strategies to optimize cash flow:

1. **Invoice and Payment Terms**: Establish clear invoice terms and payment policies to ensure timely collection of receivables. Consider offering incentives for early payment or implementing late payment penalties to encourage prompt settlements.
2. **Expense Management**: Monitor expenses closely and identify opportunities for cost savings without compromising service quality. Negotiate favorable terms with suppliers and vendors to manage cash outflows effectively.
3. **Forecasting and Planning**: Create cash flow forecasts to anticipate revenue streams and expenses over specific periods. Adjust forecasts regularly based on actual performance and market conditions to proactively manage cash flow fluctuations.

Financing Options for Growth

If additional funding is needed to expand your delivery business, explore financing options such as:

1. **Traditional Bank Loans**: Secure loans from financial institutions based on your creditworthiness and business plan. Compare

loan terms, interest rates, and repayment schedules to find the most suitable option.
2. **Small Business Administration (SBA) Loans**: SBA offers loan programs with favorable terms for small businesses, including startups. Research eligibility criteria and application requirements to apply for SBA-backed financing.
3. **Investment Capital**: Seek equity investment from angel investors, venture capitalists, or private equity firms interested in supporting innovative delivery business models. Prepare a compelling business pitch and valuation analysis to attract potential investors.

Financial Reporting and Analysis

Regular financial reporting and analysis provide insights into your delivery business's financial performance and inform strategic decision-making:

1. **Financial Statements**: Prepare accurate and comprehensive financial statements, including income statements, balance sheets, and cash flow statements. Analyze key financial ratios to assess profitability, liquidity, and operational efficiency.
2. **Performance Metrics**: Monitor performance metrics such as customer acquisition costs, average order value, and gross profit margins. Identify trends and areas for improvement to optimize financial performance and achieve business goals.
3. **Budget Variance Analysis**: Compare actual financial results against budgeted projections to identify variances and understand underlying causes. Adjust budget assumptions and strategies as needed to align with evolving business conditions.

Tax Planning and Compliance

Compliance with tax regulations is essential to avoid penalties and maintain financial integrity:

1. **Tax Obligations**: Understand federal, state, and local tax obligations for your delivery business, including income taxes, sales taxes (if applicable), payroll taxes, and quarterly estimated tax payments.
2. **Tax Deductions**: Take advantage of available tax deductions and credits for business expenses, such as vehicle expenses, depreciation, insurance premiums, and employee benefits.
3. **Professional Guidance**: Consult with a qualified accountant or tax advisor to navigate complex tax laws, maximize deductions, and ensure compliance with filing deadlines and reporting requirements.

Conclusion

Effective financial management is critical to the success and sustainability of your delivery business. By developing a comprehensive budget, implementing strategic pricing strategies, managing cash flow efficiently, exploring financing options for growth, conducting regular financial reporting and analysis, planning for taxes, you can establish a strong financial foundation for your business.

In the next chapter, we'll explore operational efficiency strategies to streamline your delivery operations, enhance productivity, and deliver exceptional service to your customers. Get ready to optimize your processes and maximize efficiency in every aspect of your delivery business.

Chapter 10: Operational Efficiency Strategies for Your Delivery Business

Welcome to Chapter 10 of your journey into starting a delivery business! In this chapter, we'll explore essential strategies to enhance operational efficiency, streamline processes, and deliver exceptional service to your customers.

Importance of Operational Efficiency

Operational efficiency is crucial for maximizing productivity, minimizing costs, and delivering superior customer experiences. By optimizing your delivery operations, you can increase profitability, improve service quality, and gain a competitive edge in the marketplace.

Streamlining Order Management

Efficient order management is the backbone of successful delivery operations. Implement these strategies to streamline the order process:

1. **Automated Order Processing**: Use delivery management software to automate order intake, processing, and assignment to drivers. This reduces manual errors, accelerates order fulfillment, and improves overall efficiency.
2. **Real-Time Order Tracking**: Provide customers with real-time tracking updates via mobile apps or online portals. Transparency in order status enhances customer satisfaction and reduces inquiries to customer support.
3. **Optimized Dispatching**: Utilize route optimization software to assign orders to drivers based on proximity, traffic conditions, and delivery time windows. Efficient dispatching minimizes delivery times and maximizes driver productivity.

Fleet Management and Vehicle Optimization

Effective fleet management is essential for maintaining vehicle reliability, minimizing downtime, and optimizing fuel efficiency:

1. **Regular Maintenance**: Schedule routine maintenance checks and inspections to ensure vehicles are in optimal condition. Address minor repairs promptly to prevent costly breakdowns and disruptions to delivery schedules.
2. **Fuel Efficiency**: Implement fuel-saving practices such as route optimization, vehicle maintenance, and driver training on eco-driving techniques. Consider investing in fuel-efficient vehicles or alternative fuel options to reduce operating costs and environmental impact.
3. **Vehicle Tracking Systems**: Install GPS tracking devices to monitor vehicle location, route adherence, and driver behavior in real-time. Tracking systems improve fleet visibility, driver accountability, and overall operational control.

Warehouse and Inventory Management

Efficient warehouse operations contribute to timely order fulfillment and inventory accuracy:

1. **Inventory Optimization**: Implement inventory management systems to track stock levels, monitor inventory turnover rates, and prevent stockouts or overstock situations. Utilize barcode scanning or RFID technology for accurate inventory tracking.
2. **Order Fulfillment Process**: Streamline picking, packing, and shipping processes to minimize fulfillment times. Organize warehouse layout for efficient product flow and storage optimization.
3. **Just-In-Time Inventory**: Adopt just-in-time inventory practices to reduce carrying costs and improve cash flow. Coordinate with suppliers to receive deliveries as needed based on demand forecasts and sales trends.

Employee Training and Development

Invest in ongoing training and development programs to empower your workforce and enhance operational efficiency:

1. **Driver Training**: Provide comprehensive training for delivery drivers on safe driving practices, customer service skills, and using delivery management software. Ensure drivers are equipped to handle various delivery scenarios and customer interactions.
2. **Continuous Improvement**: Foster a culture of continuous improvement by encouraging feedback from employees on operational processes and identifying opportunities for efficiency gains. Implement suggestions for process enhancements and recognize employee contributions.

Customer Service Excellence

Exceptional customer service is a hallmark of successful delivery businesses:

1. **Timely Communication**: Keep customers informed with proactive communication regarding order status, delays, or delivery updates. Provide multiple communication channels for customer inquiries and feedback.
2. **Flexible Delivery Options**: Offer flexible delivery options such as same-day delivery, scheduled deliveries, or express shipping to accommodate customer preferences and urgency.
3. **Problem Resolution**: Resolve customer issues promptly and professionally. Empower customer service representatives with authority to make decisions and resolve issues to customer satisfaction.

Implementing Technology Solutions

Leverage technology to automate processes, improve visibility, and enhance operational efficiency:

1. **Delivery Management Software**: Utilize integrated delivery management platforms for end-to-end order processing, route optimization, and real-time tracking. Centralized software streamlines operations and improves data accuracy.
2. **Data Analytics**: Analyze operational data to identify bottlenecks, inefficiencies, and trends. Use insights to make data-driven decisions, optimize resource allocation, and improve overall performance.

Conclusion

Operational efficiency is essential for the success and sustainability of your delivery business. By implementing strategies to streamline order management, optimize fleet operations, improve warehouse efficiency, invest in employee training, deliver exceptional customer service, and leverage technology solutions, you can enhance productivity, reduce costs, and exceed customer expectations.

In the next chapter, we'll explore strategies for scaling and expanding your delivery business. From market expansion and diversifying services to strategic partnerships and growth planning, get ready to take your delivery business to the next level of success.

Chapter 11: Scaling and Expanding Your Delivery Business

Congratulations on reaching Chapter 11 of your journey into starting a delivery business! In this chapter, we'll explore strategies for scaling and expanding your operations to capitalize on growth opportunities and achieve long-term success.

Assessing Market Expansion Opportunities

Before scaling your delivery business, conduct a thorough assessment of market expansion opportunities:

1. **Market Research**: Evaluate potential new markets based on demographic trends, consumer behavior, and demand for delivery services. Identify geographic areas with underserved or growing customer bases that align with your business goals.
2. **Competitive Analysis**: Research competitors in target markets to understand their service offerings, pricing strategies, and customer satisfaction levels. Differentiate your delivery business by offering unique value propositions or addressing unmet customer needs.
3. **Regulatory Considerations**: Consider regulatory requirements and compliance obligations in new markets, including business licensing, permits, and transportation regulations. Ensure legal compliance to avoid delays or penalties when expanding operations.

Diversifying Service Offerings

Diversifying your service offerings can attract new customers and increase revenue streams:

1. **Expanded Delivery Options**: Introduce new delivery services such as scheduled deliveries, on-demand deliveries, subscription-based services, or specialized delivery solutions for specific industries (e.g., pharmaceuticals, perishable goods).

2. **Additional Services**: Offer value-added services such as warehousing, fulfillment services, or reverse logistics (returns management) to cater to diverse customer needs and enhance competitiveness.
3. **Partnering with Businesses**: Collaborate with local businesses, e-commerce platforms, or retailers to offer integrated delivery solutions or exclusive partnerships. Leverage synergies to expand your customer base and increase service demand.

Strategic Partnerships and Alliances

Form strategic partnerships and alliances to accelerate growth and enhance operational capabilities:

1. **Supplier Partnerships**: Establish partnerships with reliable suppliers or distributors to secure preferential pricing, streamline procurement processes, and ensure timely inventory replenishment.
2. **Technology Providers**: Partner with technology providers offering innovative solutions for delivery management, route optimization, or customer engagement. Leverage technology partnerships to enhance operational efficiency and service delivery.
3. **Business Networks**: Join industry associations, trade organizations, or local business networks to access networking opportunities, industry insights, and potential collaboration with complementary businesses.

Investing in Technology and Infrastructure

Invest in technology and infrastructure to support scalable growth and operational efficiency:

1. **Scalable Technology Solutions**: Upgrade delivery management software, fleet tracking systems, and IT infrastructure to handle increased transaction volumes and expand service capabilities.

2. **Logistics Optimization**: Implement advanced analytics, AI-powered forecasting tools, or blockchain technology for supply chain transparency and operational optimization. Leverage data-driven insights to improve decision-making and resource allocation.
3. **Infrastructure Expansion**: Expand warehouse capacity, distribution centers, or fulfillment facilities to accommodate growing inventory and increase operational flexibility. Invest in sustainable practices and energy-efficient facilities to support long-term growth.

Financial Planning for Growth

Develop a strategic financial plan to support expansion initiatives and manage capital allocation effectively:

1. **Capital Investment**: Evaluate funding options such as equity financing, bank loans, or business lines of credit to fund expansion projects, acquire assets, or invest in technology upgrades.
2. **Financial Forecasting**: Create detailed financial projections, including revenue forecasts, expense budgets, and cash flow analysis. Monitor key performance indicators (KPIs) to track progress towards growth objectives and adjust strategies as needed.
3. **Risk Management**: Assess potential risks associated with expansion, such as market volatility, regulatory changes, or operational challenges. Develop risk mitigation strategies and contingency plans to safeguard against unforeseen circumstances.

Scaling Operations Efficiently

Implement strategies to scale operations efficiently while maintaining service quality and customer satisfaction:

1. **Operational Scalability**: Standardize processes, implement scalable workflows, and establish clear protocols for training new employees or onboarding new clients. Anticipate growth-related challenges and proactively address operational bottlenecks.
2. **Customer Relationship Management**: Enhance customer service capabilities, invest in CRM systems, and personalize customer interactions to retain loyal customers and foster long-term relationships.
3. **Feedback and Adaptation**: Solicit feedback from customers, employees, and stakeholders to continuously improve service offerings, address emerging needs, and adapt to evolving market dynamics.

Conclusion

Scaling and expanding your delivery business requires careful planning, strategic partnerships, technological investments, and financial foresight. By assessing market expansion opportunities, diversifying service offerings, forming strategic alliances, investing in technology and infrastructure, planning for financial growth, and scaling operations efficiently, you can position your delivery business for sustainable growth and market leadership.

In the next chapter, we'll explore the importance of sustainability practices in the delivery industry. From eco-friendly initiatives to corporate social responsibility (CSR), discover how adopting sustainable practices can benefit your business, community, and the environment.

Chapter 12: Embracing Sustainability in Your Delivery Business

Welcome to Chapter 12 of your journey into starting a delivery business! In this chapter, we'll explore the importance of embracing sustainability practices to minimize environmental impact, enhance brand reputation, and contribute to a sustainable future.

Understanding Sustainability in Delivery Services

Sustainability in the delivery industry involves minimizing carbon emissions, reducing waste, conserving resources, and promoting environmental stewardship. As consumer awareness and regulatory pressures increase, integrating sustainable practices into your business operations is not only beneficial for the planet but also essential for long-term business viability.

Adopting Eco-Friendly Delivery Practices

1. **Alternative Fuel Vehicles**: Consider transitioning to electric, hybrid, or compressed natural gas (CNG) vehicles to reduce greenhouse gas emissions and air pollution. Explore government incentives or subsidies for eco-friendly vehicle purchases.
2. **Route Optimization**: Implement route optimization software to minimize mileage, fuel consumption, and carbon emissions. Efficient route planning reduces environmental impact while improving operational efficiency.
3. **Vehicle Maintenance**: Maintain vehicles regularly to ensure optimal performance and fuel efficiency. Proper maintenance reduces emissions and extends vehicle lifespan, lowering overall environmental footprint.

Sustainable Packaging Solutions

1. **Recyclable Materials**: Use recyclable packaging materials such as cardboard, paper, or biodegradable plastics. Minimize single-

use plastics and opt for materials that can be easily recycled or reused by customers.
2. **Minimalist Packaging**: Adopt minimalist packaging practices to reduce material waste and packaging volume. Optimize packaging sizes to fit products snugly, minimizing excess space and materials.
3. **Reusable Packaging Options**: Offer reusable packaging options or incentivize customers to return packaging for reuse or recycling. Collaborate with suppliers to source eco-friendly packaging solutions.

Efficient Logistics and Supply Chain Management

1. **Supply Chain Transparency**: Partner with suppliers committed to sustainable practices and ethical sourcing. Prioritize suppliers with certifications such as Fair Trade, organic, or sustainable forestry practices.
2. **Local Sourcing**: Source materials and products locally whenever possible to reduce transportation-related emissions and support local economies. Consider establishing partnerships with local producers or distributors.
3. **Reverse Logistics**: Implement efficient reverse logistics processes for product returns, recycling, or refurbishment. Minimize waste through product reuse, recycling programs, or responsible disposal practices.

Energy Efficiency Initiatives

1. **Energy-Efficient Facilities**: Upgrade to energy-efficient lighting, HVAC systems, and appliances in warehouses, offices, and delivery hubs. Install motion sensors or timers to optimize energy usage and reduce operational costs.
2. **Renewable Energy Sources**: Invest in renewable energy sources such as solar panels or wind turbines to power facilities or recharge electric vehicles. Reduce reliance on fossil fuels and lower carbon emissions associated with energy consumption.

3. **Energy Conservation Practices**: Promote energy conservation among employees through training programs, awareness campaigns, and workplace policies. Encourage simple actions such as turning off lights and equipment when not in use to conserve energy.

Corporate Social Responsibility (CSR) and Community Engagement

1. **Community Partnerships**: Engage with local communities through volunteer programs, charitable donations, or sponsorship of environmental initiatives. Build positive relationships and demonstrate commitment to social and environmental responsibility.
2. **Transparent Reporting**: Communicate your sustainability efforts and progress openly with stakeholders, including customers, employees, investors, and regulatory bodies. Publish annual sustainability reports detailing achievements, goals, and initiatives.
3. **Employee Involvement**: Foster a culture of sustainability among employees by encouraging participation in green initiatives, recycling programs, or community clean-up events. Empower employees to contribute ideas and initiatives for improving sustainability practices within the organization.

Measuring and Reporting Sustainability Impact

1. **Key Performance Indicators (KPIs)**: Establish measurable KPIs to track environmental impact, such as carbon footprint reduction, waste diversion rates, energy consumption per delivery, and sustainable packaging adoption.
2. **Life Cycle Assessments**: Conduct life cycle assessments (LCAs) to evaluate the environmental impacts of products, services, or operational processes. Use findings to identify opportunities for improvement and prioritize sustainable alternatives.
3. **Continuous Improvement**: Commit to continuous improvement in sustainability practices through regular review, assessment,

and adaptation of strategies. Stay informed about industry best practices, technological advancements, and regulatory changes affecting sustainability.

Conclusion

Embracing sustainability in your delivery business is not only a moral imperative but also a strategic opportunity to differentiate your brand, attract environmentally conscious customers, and contribute positively to the planet. By adopting eco-friendly delivery practices, implementing sustainable packaging solutions, optimizing logistics and supply chain management, investing in energy efficiency initiatives, practicing corporate social responsibility, measuring impact, and fostering a culture of sustainability, you can create a greener and more resilient future for your business and communities.

In the next chapter, we'll explore the future trends and innovations shaping the delivery industry. From drone delivery and autonomous vehicles to AI-powered logistics and green technologies, discover how technological advancements are revolutionizing the delivery landscape.

Chapter 13: Future Trends and Innovations in the Delivery Industry

Welcome to Chapter 13 of your journey into starting a delivery business! In this chapter, we'll explore exciting future trends and innovations shaping the delivery industry. Staying informed about these developments can help you anticipate changes, adapt your strategies, and stay ahead in a competitive marketplace.

Technological Advancements

1. **Drone Delivery**: The concept of drone delivery is gaining traction, promising faster and more efficient deliveries, especially in urban areas. Drones can navigate traffic and deliver small packages directly to customers' doorsteps, reducing delivery times and operational costs.
2. **Autonomous Vehicles**: Self-driving vehicles are poised to revolutionize last-mile delivery. Companies are investing in autonomous technologies to enhance delivery efficiency, reduce labor costs, and improve safety. These vehicles can operate round-the-clock, optimizing delivery schedules and customer convenience.
3. **AI-Powered Logistics**: Artificial Intelligence (AI) is transforming logistics with predictive analytics, demand forecasting, and route optimization. AI algorithms analyze vast amounts of data to optimize delivery routes, predict customer demand, and improve operational efficiency.

Sustainability Initiatives

1. **Green Technologies**: The shift towards eco-friendly delivery solutions continues with electric vehicles, hydrogen-powered trucks, and sustainable packaging materials. Companies are adopting carbon-neutral practices to reduce environmental impact and meet regulatory requirements.
2. **Circular Economy Practices**: Embracing circular economy principles involves reducing waste, reusing materials, and recycling packaging. Businesses are exploring closed-loop

systems where packaging materials are returned, refurbished, or repurposed, minimizing environmental footprint.
3. **Carbon Offsetting Programs**: Many delivery companies are implementing carbon offsetting programs to neutralize emissions from transportation activities. By investing in renewable energy projects or reforestation initiatives, businesses can balance their carbon footprint and promote environmental stewardship.

Customer Experience Enhancements

1. **Real-Time Tracking and Notifications**: Customers expect transparency and real-time updates on their deliveries. Advanced tracking systems, mobile apps, and SMS notifications keep customers informed about delivery status, estimated arrival times, and any delays.
2. **Personalized Delivery Options**: Personalization is key to enhancing customer satisfaction. Businesses are offering flexible delivery options such as same-day delivery, evening delivery slots, or delivery to alternative locations specified by customers.
3. **Contactless Delivery Solutions**: The COVID-19 pandemic accelerated the adoption of contactless delivery options. Customers appreciate contactless drop-offs, where packages are left securely at their doorstep or designated locations, minimizing physical interaction.

E-Commerce Integration

1. **Rise of Online Shopping**: The growth of e-commerce continues to drive demand for efficient delivery services. Businesses are integrating seamlessly with online platforms, marketplaces, and retail stores to fulfill orders and reach a broader customer base.
2. **Omni-Channel Strategies**: Omni-channel retailing combines online and offline channels, offering customers multiple ways to shop and receive deliveries. Delivery businesses are adapting to support omni-channel strategies with flexible fulfillment options and seamless customer experiences.

3. **Reverse Logistics Optimization**: Managing returns efficiently is essential in e-commerce. Companies are investing in reverse logistics solutions to handle product returns, exchanges, and refunds seamlessly, minimizing costs and improving customer satisfaction.

Data-Driven Decision Making

1. **Predictive Analytics**: Harnessing big data and predictive analytics allows delivery businesses to anticipate customer demand, optimize inventory management, and plan efficient delivery routes. Data-driven insights inform strategic decisions and improve operational efficiency.
2. **Customer Insights**: Analyzing customer behavior and preferences helps businesses tailor services, personalize marketing campaigns, and enhance overall customer experience. Understanding customer demographics, shopping patterns, and feedback guides business strategies.
3. **Operational Efficiency**: Data analytics optimize resource allocation, fleet management, and workforce productivity. Continuous monitoring of key performance indicators (KPIs) identifies areas for improvement, streamlines operations, and reduces costs.

Regulatory and Compliance Landscape

1. **Regulatory Changes**: Stay informed about evolving regulations affecting the delivery industry, including safety standards, environmental regulations, and data privacy laws. Compliance ensures operational continuity and mitigates legal risks.
2. **Ethical Considerations**: Address ethical considerations such as data security, responsible sourcing, and fair labor practices. Upholding ethical standards builds trust with customers, employees, and stakeholders, enhancing brand reputation.
3. **Adaptation Strategies**: Develop adaptive strategies to navigate regulatory changes and market disruptions. Proactively engage

with industry associations, government agencies, and legal advisors to stay compliant and advocate for industry interests.

Conclusion

The delivery industry is evolving rapidly with technological innovations, sustainability initiatives, enhanced customer experiences, and data-driven decision-making. By embracing future trends and innovations, delivery businesses can drive growth, improve operational efficiency, and meet evolving customer expectations. Stay proactive, adapt to change, and leverage emerging technologies to position your business for success in the dynamic delivery landscape.

In the next chapter, we'll explore the importance of workforce management and employee engagement in optimizing delivery operations. From recruiting and training to retaining talent and fostering a positive work culture, discover strategies to build a motivated and efficient delivery team.

Chapter 14: Workforce Management and Employee Engagement in Your Delivery Business

Welcome to Chapter 14 of your journey into starting a delivery business! In this chapter, we'll delve into the critical aspects of workforce management and employee engagement. Building a motivated and efficient team is essential for delivering exceptional service, optimizing operations, and fostering long-term success.

Importance of Workforce Management

Effective workforce management involves recruiting, training, scheduling, and retaining skilled employees who contribute to the overall success of your delivery business:

1. **Recruitment Strategies**: Develop targeted recruitment strategies to attract candidates with relevant skills and experience in delivery operations. Utilize online job boards, social media platforms, and industry networks to reach potential candidates.
2. **Training and Development**: Provide comprehensive training programs for delivery drivers and warehouse staff. Training should cover safety protocols, customer service standards, operational procedures, and the use of delivery management software.
3. **Scheduling Optimization**: Implement efficient scheduling practices to align workforce availability with delivery demand. Utilize scheduling software to manage shifts, routes, and driver assignments effectively, ensuring optimal coverage and productivity.

Creating a Positive Work Culture

A positive work culture enhances employee satisfaction, boosts morale, and increases productivity:

1. **Clear Communication**: Foster open communication channels between management and employees. Keep team members informed about company goals, performance expectations, and operational updates through regular meetings, newsletters, or digital platforms.
2. **Recognition and Rewards**: Acknowledge employee contributions and achievements through formal recognition programs, incentives, or performance-based bonuses. Celebrate milestones, birthdays, and team successes to build camaraderie and motivate employees.
3. **Work-Life Balance**: Support work-life balance by offering flexible scheduling options, paid time off, and family-friendly policies. Prioritize employee well-being and mental health to maintain job satisfaction and reduce turnover.

Team Building and Collaboration

Promote teamwork and collaboration among delivery teams to enhance efficiency and customer service:

1. **Cross-Training**: Cross-train employees in different roles or tasks within the delivery operation. Versatile team members can fill in during peak periods, vacations, or unexpected absences, ensuring continuity of service.
2. **Collaborative Environment**: Encourage collaboration between drivers, warehouse staff, and customer service representatives. Foster a team-oriented culture where employees support each other, share best practices, and work towards common goals.
3. **Feedback Mechanisms**: Solicit feedback from employees on operational processes, equipment usability, and customer interactions. Act on constructive feedback to improve workflow efficiency, address concerns, and enhance job satisfaction.

Empowering Employee Safety and Well-Being

Prioritize employee safety and well-being to maintain a healthy and productive workforce:

1. **Safety Protocols**: Establish stringent safety protocols for vehicle operation, loading and unloading procedures, and workplace ergonomics. Conduct regular safety training sessions and inspections to prevent accidents and injuries.
2. **Health Benefits and Resources**: Offer comprehensive health benefits, including medical insurance, wellness programs, and access to healthcare resources. Promote preventive care and provide resources for mental health support.
3. **Employee Assistance Programs (EAP)**: Implement EAPs to offer confidential counseling, financial assistance, and resources for personal or work-related challenges. Support employees facing stress, burnout, or life transitions to enhance overall well-being.

Performance Management and Feedback

Implement performance management strategies to assess employee performance, provide feedback, and support professional growth:

1. **Performance Reviews**: Conduct regular performance reviews to evaluate employee performance against established goals and competencies. Provide constructive feedback, recognize achievements, and identify areas for improvement.
2. **Professional Development**: Support career advancement through training opportunities, skill development workshops, and tuition reimbursement programs. Encourage employees to pursue certifications or specialized training relevant to their roles.
3. **Goal Setting**: Collaboratively set SMART (Specific, Measurable, Achievable, Relevant, Time-bound) goals with employees to align individual objectives with organizational priorities. Monitor progress, adjust goals as needed, and celebrate milestones together.

Embracing Diversity and Inclusion

Create a diverse and inclusive workplace culture that values and respects employees' unique backgrounds, perspectives, and contributions:

1. **Diversity Initiatives**: Implement diversity recruitment strategies and policies that promote equal opportunities for all candidates. Cultivate a workplace culture where diversity is celebrated, and inclusivity is embedded in organizational values.
2. **Training on Cultural Competence**: Provide training on cultural competence, unconscious bias, and respectful communication. Foster an inclusive environment where all employees feel valued, heard, and empowered to contribute their best work.
3. **Community Engagement**: Engage in community initiatives and partnerships that support diversity, equity, and inclusion. Collaborate with local organizations, participate in events, and advocate for social justice issues to make a positive impact beyond the workplace.

Conclusion

Workforce management and employee engagement are integral to the success and sustainability of your delivery business. By prioritizing recruitment, training, scheduling optimization, fostering a positive work culture, promoting teamwork and collaboration, ensuring employee safety and well-being, implementing performance management strategies, embracing diversity and inclusion, you can build a motivated and resilient team that drives operational excellence and delivers outstanding service to customers.

In the next chapter, we'll explore customer retention strategies and loyalty programs to cultivate lasting relationships, enhance customer satisfaction, and stimulate business growth. Discover how personalized experiences and customer-centric approaches can differentiate your delivery business in a competitive marketplace.

Chapter 15: Customer Retention Strategies and Building Loyalty in Your Delivery Business

Welcome to Chapter 15 of your journey into starting a delivery business! In this chapter, we'll explore effective strategies for retaining customers, building loyalty, and cultivating lasting relationships. Customer retention is crucial for sustainable growth, profitability, and maintaining a competitive edge in the delivery industry.

Understanding Customer Retention

Customer retention refers to the ability of a business to retain existing customers over time by delivering value, fostering loyalty, and exceeding expectations:

1. **Importance of Customer Retention**: Retaining loyal customers is more cost-effective than acquiring new ones. Loyal customers tend to spend more, refer others to your business, and provide valuable feedback that can drive business improvements.
2. **Lifetime Value**: Focus on maximizing the lifetime value of customers by nurturing relationships, delivering exceptional service, and anticipating their needs. Long-term customers contribute significantly to revenue and business sustainability.
3. **Customer Experience**: A positive customer experience is pivotal in retention efforts. From seamless order fulfillment to responsive customer support, every interaction shapes perceptions and influences customer loyalty.

Personalized Customer Experiences

1. **Segmentation and Targeting**: Segment customers based on demographics, purchase behavior, and preferences. Tailor marketing messages, promotions, and service offerings to meet the unique needs of different customer segments.
2. **Personalized Communication**: Use customer data to personalize communication through email marketing, SMS notifications, or

personalized offers. Address customers by name, acknowledge their preferences, and anticipate their next purchase.
3. **Feedback and Listening**: Actively seek feedback from customers through surveys, reviews, and social media channels. Use insights to improve service delivery, address concerns promptly, and demonstrate responsiveness to customer input.

Building Customer Loyalty Programs

1. **Loyalty Rewards**: Implement a tiered loyalty program where customers earn points, discounts, or exclusive perks based on their purchase frequency or spending levels. Reward loyal customers for their continued patronage and incentivize repeat business.
2. **Referral Programs**: Encourage satisfied customers to refer friends and family through referral incentives or discounts. Word-of-mouth recommendations from loyal customers can significantly impact new customer acquisition and retention.
3. **Special Promotions and Offers**: Surprise loyal customers with special promotions, early access to new products, or personalized birthday discounts. Create memorable experiences that reinforce their decision to choose your delivery service.

Proactive Customer Service

1. **Responsive Support**: Provide timely and empathetic customer support through multiple channels, including phone, email, and live chat. Resolve issues promptly, escalate concerns when necessary, and follow up to ensure customer satisfaction.
2. **Proactive Communication**: Keep customers informed about order status, delivery updates, and any potential delays. Provide real-time tracking links or notifications to enhance transparency and manage expectations.
3. **Customer Education**: Educate customers about your delivery processes, service options, and how they can maximize benefits from using your service. Empower customers to make informed

decisions and feel confident in their interactions with your brand.

Continuous Improvement and Adaptation

1. **Feedback Loop**: Use customer feedback to identify areas for improvement and innovate service offerings. Act on constructive feedback to refine processes, enhance product offerings, and exceed customer expectations.
2. **Adaptability**: Stay agile and responsive to market trends, customer preferences, and competitive pressures. Anticipate industry shifts, technological advancements, and evolving consumer behaviors to adapt your retention strategies accordingly.
3. **Competitive Analysis**: Monitor competitor strategies, pricing models, and customer retention tactics. Differentiate your delivery business by offering unique value propositions, superior service quality, and personalized customer experiences.

Measuring Customer Retention Success

1. **Key Metrics**: Track key performance indicators (KPIs) such as customer retention rate, repeat purchase rate, Net Promoter Score (NPS), and customer lifetime value (CLV). Analyze trends over time to gauge the effectiveness of retention strategies.
2. **Customer Satisfaction Surveys**: Conduct regular customer satisfaction surveys to assess overall satisfaction levels, identify areas for improvement, and measure the impact of retention initiatives on customer loyalty.
3. **Data Analytics**: Utilize data analytics tools to gain actionable insights into customer behavior, preferences, and purchasing patterns. Leverage predictive analytics to forecast customer churn and proactively implement retention strategies.

Conclusion

Customer retention is a cornerstone of business success in the delivery industry. By prioritizing personalized customer experiences, building loyalty through rewards programs, providing proactive customer service, continuously improving based on feedback, and measuring retention success through key metrics, you can cultivate loyal customers who advocate for your brand and contribute to sustainable growth.

In the next chapter, we'll explore crisis management strategies for handling unexpected challenges, disruptions, and emergencies in your delivery business. From contingency planning and communication protocols to maintaining operational resilience, learn how to navigate crises effectively and safeguard your business reputation.

Chapter 16: Crisis Management Strategies for Your Delivery Business

Welcome to Chapter 16 of your journey into starting a delivery business! In this chapter, we'll delve into essential crisis management strategies to effectively navigate unexpected challenges, disruptions, and emergencies. Developing a proactive approach to crisis management is crucial for maintaining business continuity, safeguarding your reputation, and ensuring customer satisfaction.

Understanding Crisis Management

Crisis management involves identifying potential risks, preparing response plans, and implementing strategies to mitigate impact during emergencies or disruptions:

1. **Types of Crises**: Crises in the delivery industry can range from natural disasters and extreme weather events to transportation accidents, supplier failures, or cybersecurity breaches. Each crisis requires a tailored response to minimize disruption and protect stakeholders.
2. **Importance of Preparedness**: Proactive preparation and readiness can mitigate risks, reduce recovery time, and uphold business operations. Establishing clear protocols, communication strategies, and contingency plans is essential for effective crisis management.
3. **Stakeholder Engagement**: Engage with internal teams, external partners, customers, and regulatory authorities to coordinate efforts, share information, and maintain transparency throughout the crisis management process.

Developing a Crisis Management Plan

1. **Risk Assessment**: Conduct a comprehensive risk assessment to identify potential threats and vulnerabilities specific to your delivery business. Prioritize risks based on likelihood and potential impact to prioritize mitigation efforts.

2. **Response Protocols**: Establish clear protocols and procedures for responding to different types of crises. Define roles and responsibilities within your crisis management team, including decision-makers, communicators, and operational responders.
3. **Communication Strategies**: Develop robust communication strategies to disseminate timely and accurate information to internal stakeholders, customers, media, and the public. Maintain open lines of communication throughout the crisis to manage expectations and address concerns proactively.

Key Elements of a Crisis Management Plan

1. **Emergency Response Procedures**: Outline step-by-step procedures for responding to emergencies, including evacuation protocols, first aid procedures, and emergency contacts. Ensure all employees are trained in emergency response and aware of their roles.
2. **Business Continuity Plans**: Develop business continuity plans (BCPs) to ensure critical operations can resume quickly following a crisis. Identify alternate suppliers, backup facilities, and IT recovery strategies to minimize downtime and maintain service delivery.
3. **Data Security and IT Resilience**: Implement robust cybersecurity measures to protect sensitive data and IT systems from cyber threats or breaches. Backup data regularly, implement encryption protocols, and test IT disaster recovery plans to safeguard business continuity.

Crisis Communication Strategies

1. **Transparent and Timely Communication**: During a crisis, prioritize transparency and provide regular updates to stakeholders. Communicate honestly about the situation, actions being taken, and expected outcomes to build trust and credibility.
2. **Media Relations**: Designate a spokesperson or media relations team to handle inquiries from journalists and reporters. Prepare

key messages, press releases, and media statements in advance to ensure consistent messaging and manage public perception.
3. **Customer Communication**: Proactively notify customers about service disruptions, delays, or changes in delivery schedules. Provide alternative solutions, such as rerouting shipments or offering compensation, to minimize inconvenience and maintain customer loyalty.

Training and Preparedness Exercises

1. **Simulation Exercises**: Conduct regular crisis simulation exercises or tabletop drills to test the effectiveness of your crisis management plan. Evaluate team responses, identify gaps, and update protocols based on lessons learned.
2. **Employee Training**: Train employees on crisis response procedures, including situational awareness, emergency communication protocols, and escalation procedures. Empower employees to take decisive actions and prioritize safety during emergencies.
3. **Continuous Improvement**: Continuously review and update your crisis management plan based on feedback, changing risks, and industry best practices. Stay informed about emerging threats and adapt strategies to enhance preparedness and resilience.

Maintaining Stakeholder Trust and Reputation

1. **Ethical Considerations**: Uphold ethical standards and integrity in all crisis management activities. Demonstrate accountability, empathy, and a commitment to resolving issues promptly to maintain stakeholder trust and preserve your brand reputation.
2. **Post-Crisis Evaluation**: Conduct a thorough debriefing and post-crisis evaluation to assess response effectiveness, identify areas for improvement, and implement corrective actions. Communicate lessons learned internally to strengthen future crisis preparedness.

3. **Community Engagement**: Engage with local communities, customers, and stakeholders to demonstrate your commitment to safety, resilience, and responsible business practices. Build goodwill through community outreach initiatives and support during recovery efforts.

Conclusion

Effective crisis management is essential for protecting your delivery business from unforeseen disruptions, maintaining operational continuity, and safeguarding stakeholder trust. By developing a comprehensive crisis management plan, prioritizing preparedness, implementing robust communication strategies, training employees, and continuously improving based on feedback and evaluation, you can navigate crises with confidence and resilience.

In the next chapter, we'll explore emerging technologies and innovations reshaping the delivery industry. From artificial intelligence and autonomous vehicles to sustainable logistics solutions, discover how technological advancements can drive efficiency, enhance customer experiences, and propel your delivery business forward in a rapidly evolving marketplace.

Chapter 17: Emerging Technologies in the Delivery Industry

Welcome to Chapter 17 of your journey into starting a delivery business! In this chapter, we'll explore the exciting world of emerging technologies reshaping the delivery industry. Keeping abreast of these innovations can revolutionize your operations, enhance efficiency, and improve customer satisfaction.

The Impact of Emerging Technologies

1. **Artificial Intelligence (AI)**: AI-powered solutions are transforming delivery logistics with predictive analytics, route optimization, and demand forecasting. Machine learning algorithms analyze data to improve delivery efficiency, reduce costs, and enhance decision-making processes.
2. **Internet of Things (IoT)**: IoT devices such as sensors and smart trackers monitor package location, temperature, and environmental conditions in real-time. IoT-enabled logistics enhance visibility, reduce theft, and ensure timely delivery by tracking assets throughout the supply chain.
3. **Blockchain Technology**: Blockchain enhances transparency and security in supply chain management by creating immutable records of transactions. Smart contracts automate processes, verify delivery authenticity, and streamline payments between parties.

Autonomous Vehicles and Drones

1. **Autonomous Delivery Vehicles**: Self-driving vehicles are revolutionizing last-mile delivery. These vehicles navigate urban environments, optimize routes, and reduce delivery times while minimizing labor costs and improving safety.
2. **Drone Delivery**: Drones enable rapid and cost-effective delivery of small packages to remote or hard-to-reach locations. Drone technology enhances delivery speed, reduces carbon emissions, and expands delivery capabilities in urban and rural areas.

Sustainable Logistics Solutions

1. **Electric and Hybrid Vehicles**: Transitioning to electric and hybrid vehicles reduces carbon emissions and operational costs. Governments incentivize eco-friendly vehicle adoption through subsidies, tax breaks, and infrastructure development.
2. **Alternative Fuels**: Biofuels, hydrogen-powered vehicles, and compressed natural gas (CNG) offer sustainable alternatives to traditional fossil fuels. These fuels lower greenhouse gas emissions and support environmental sustainability initiatives.

Augmented Reality (AR) and Virtual Reality (VR)

1. **AR for Warehousing**: AR technology improves warehouse efficiency by providing real-time inventory updates, guiding picking processes, and reducing errors. AR-enabled smart glasses enhance worker productivity and accuracy during order fulfillment.
2. **VR for Training**: Virtual Reality simulations offer immersive training experiences for delivery drivers and warehouse staff. VR training modules simulate real-world scenarios, improve safety awareness, and enhance operational readiness.

Predictive Analytics and Big Data

1. **Predictive Analytics**: Predictive models analyze historical data to forecast customer demand, optimize inventory management, and predict delivery routes. These insights enable proactive decision-making and enhance supply chain efficiency.
2. **Big Data Integration**: Integrating big data from multiple sources enhances visibility across the supply chain. Real-time data analytics improve decision-making, mitigate risks, and optimize resource allocation for efficient delivery operations.

Customer Experience Innovations

1. **Real-Time Tracking**: Advanced tracking technologies provide customers with real-time updates on delivery status, estimated arrival times, and driver location. Real-time tracking enhances transparency and improves customer satisfaction.
2. **Contactless Delivery**: Contactless delivery options minimize physical contact between customers and delivery personnel, enhancing safety and convenience. Customers appreciate secure drop-off solutions and personalized delivery preferences.

Implementation Challenges and Considerations

1. **Regulatory Compliance**: Navigating regulatory frameworks and compliance requirements for emerging technologies can be complex. Stay informed about local regulations, privacy laws, and safety standards when adopting new technologies.
2. **Integration with Existing Systems**: Seamless integration of emerging technologies with existing IT infrastructure and operational processes requires careful planning and investment in compatible systems and training.

Investing in Innovation

1. **Strategic Partnerships**: Collaborate with technology providers, startups, and industry partners to pilot new technologies and leverage expertise. Strategic partnerships accelerate innovation, reduce implementation risks, and drive competitive advantage.
2. **Continuous Learning and Adaptation**: Embrace a culture of innovation and continuous learning within your organization. Stay abreast of technological advancements, industry trends, and consumer preferences to remain competitive in the evolving delivery landscape.

Conclusion

Embracing emerging technologies in your delivery business can revolutionize operations, enhance efficiency, and elevate customer experiences. By adopting AI-powered logistics solutions, leveraging autonomous vehicles and drones, implementing sustainable practices, harnessing AR/VR for training, utilizing predictive analytics, and prioritizing customer-centric innovations, you can position your business for growth and success in a rapidly evolving marketplace.

In the next chapter, we'll explore strategic marketing strategies to attract new customers, differentiate your delivery services, and build a strong brand presence. Discover effective marketing tactics, customer acquisition channels, and branding strategies to drive business growth and expand your market reach.

Chapter 18: Strategic Marketing for Your Delivery Business

Welcome to Chapter 18 of your journey into starting a delivery business! In this chapter, we'll delve into strategic marketing strategies that can help you attract new customers, differentiate your services, and build a strong brand presence. Effective marketing is essential for driving business growth, expanding your market reach, and maintaining a competitive edge.

Understanding Your Market

1. **Market Research**: Begin with thorough market research to understand the dynamics of the delivery industry in your target area. Identify market trends, customer preferences, and the competitive landscape. Use surveys, focus groups, and online research to gather valuable insights.
2. **Customer Segmentation**: Segment your target market based on demographics, geographic location, buying behavior, and needs. Create detailed customer personas to tailor your marketing messages and services to specific segments effectively.
3. **Competitive Analysis**: Analyze your competitors' strengths and weaknesses. Identify what they offer, their pricing strategies, and their marketing tactics. Use this information to differentiate your services and find opportunities to fill gaps in the market.

Building Your Brand

1. **Brand Identity**: Develop a strong brand identity that reflects your business values, mission, and unique selling propositions (USPs). Your brand identity includes your business name, logo, color scheme, and overall aesthetic. Ensure it resonates with your target audience.
2. **Brand Story**: Craft a compelling brand story that communicates your journey, values, and what sets you apart from competitors. Share this story across your marketing channels to build a personal connection with your audience.

3. **Consistency**: Maintain consistency in your branding across all touchpoints, including your website, social media, packaging, and customer communications. Consistency reinforces brand recognition and trust.

Effective Marketing Channels

1. **Digital Marketing**: Leverage digital marketing channels to reach a broader audience. This includes search engine optimization (SEO), pay-per-click (PPC) advertising, email marketing, and content marketing. Focus on creating valuable content that addresses your customers' needs and interests.
2. **Social Media Marketing**: Use social media platforms such as Facebook, Instagram, Twitter, and LinkedIn to engage with your audience, share updates, and promote your services. Run targeted ad campaigns to reach specific customer segments.
3. **Local Marketing**: Implement local marketing strategies to attract customers in your delivery area. This can include local SEO, Google My Business listings, and partnerships with local businesses. Attend community events and sponsor local initiatives to increase brand visibility.

Customer Acquisition Strategies

1. **Referral Programs**: Encourage satisfied customers to refer friends and family by offering referral incentives, such as discounts or free services. Word-of-mouth referrals are a powerful way to acquire new customers.
2. **Promotions and Discounts**: Run special promotions and discounts to attract new customers. Limited-time offers, first-time customer discounts, and bundled services can entice potential customers to try your delivery service.
3. **Partnerships**: Form strategic partnerships with local businesses, e-commerce stores, and restaurants to offer integrated delivery solutions. Partnerships can provide a steady stream of customers and expand your market reach.

Enhancing Customer Engagement

1. **Personalized Marketing**: Use customer data to personalize marketing messages and offers. Address customers by name, recommend services based on their previous purchases, and send personalized emails to enhance customer engagement.
2. **Loyalty Programs**: Implement a loyalty program that rewards repeat customers with points, discounts, or exclusive perks. Loyalty programs encourage repeat business and foster long-term customer relationships.
3. **Customer Feedback**: Actively seek and respond to customer feedback. Use surveys, reviews, and social media interactions to gather insights into customer satisfaction and areas for improvement. Show customers that you value their opinions by acting on their feedback.

Measuring Marketing Success

1. **Key Performance Indicators (KPIs)**: Identify and track KPIs to measure the success of your marketing efforts. Common KPIs include customer acquisition cost (CAC), customer lifetime value (CLV), conversion rates, and return on investment (ROI).
2. **Analytics Tools**: Use analytics tools such as Google Analytics, social media insights, and email marketing platforms to monitor the performance of your marketing campaigns. Analyze data to identify trends, optimize strategies, and make data-driven decisions.
3. **Regular Reviews**: Conduct regular reviews of your marketing strategies to assess their effectiveness. Adjust your tactics based on performance data, market changes, and customer feedback to continuously improve your marketing efforts.

Conclusion

Strategic marketing is crucial for the success and growth of your delivery business. By understanding your market, building a strong brand, leveraging effective marketing channels, implementing customer acquisition strategies, enhancing customer engagement, and measuring marketing success, you can attract new customers, build loyalty, and differentiate your services in a competitive marketplace.

In the next chapter, we'll explore the financial management aspects of running a delivery business. Learn how to manage your finances, control costs, and optimize profitability to ensure long-term sustainability and growth.

Chapter 19: Financial Management for Your Delivery Business

Welcome to Chapter 19 of your journey into starting a delivery business! This chapter focuses on the critical aspect of financial management. Proper financial management is the backbone of a successful business, ensuring sustainability, growth, and profitability. In this chapter, we'll delve into budgeting, cost control, financial planning, and profit optimization in a detailed and approachable manner.

The Importance of Financial Management

1. **Sustainability**: Good financial management ensures your business can survive and thrive over the long term. It helps you understand your cash flow, manage expenses, and plan for future growth.
2. **Profitability**: Keeping a close eye on finances allows you to identify profitable services and areas where you can cut costs, boosting your overall profit margins.
3. **Decision-Making**: Financial data is crucial for making informed business decisions. From pricing strategies to expansion plans, having a clear financial picture guides your choices.

Budgeting and Forecasting

1. **Creating a Budget**: Start by creating a detailed budget that outlines your expected income and expenses. Consider all aspects of your delivery business, including vehicle maintenance, fuel, salaries, marketing, and technology costs.
2. **Income Projections**: Estimate your income based on market research and historical data. Include different revenue streams like delivery fees, partnerships, and additional services.
3. **Expense Tracking**: Track your expenses meticulously. Categorize them into fixed costs (rent, salaries) and variable costs (fuel, maintenance). Use budgeting software to streamline this process.

4. **Forecasting**: Regularly update your financial forecasts based on actual performance and market changes. Adjust your budget as needed to reflect new realities and opportunities.

Managing Cash Flow

1. **Understanding Cash Flow**: Cash flow is the movement of money in and out of your business. Positive cash flow means more money is coming in than going out, which is essential for operational stability.
2. **Cash Flow Statement**: Maintain a cash flow statement to monitor your financial health. This statement helps you understand how much cash is available to cover expenses, invest in growth, or save for future needs.
3. **Invoicing and Collections**: Implement efficient invoicing and collections processes to ensure timely payments from clients. Use digital invoicing tools to track outstanding invoices and send reminders.
4. **Managing Surpluses and Shortfalls**: Plan for surplus cash by investing in growth opportunities or saving for future needs. Prepare for cash shortfalls by having a line of credit or an emergency fund.

Cost Control and Reduction

1. **Identifying Costs**: Break down all costs associated with your delivery business. This includes direct costs like fuel and driver wages, and indirect costs like marketing and administrative expenses.
2. **Cost Analysis**: Regularly review your costs to identify areas where you can reduce expenses. For example, negotiate better rates with suppliers, optimize delivery routes to save fuel, or explore cheaper marketing channels.
3. **Efficiency Improvements**: Implement technology and process improvements to enhance efficiency. GPS routing software, automated scheduling, and digital tracking can reduce operational costs and improve service quality.

4. **Variable Costs Management**: Keep a close eye on variable costs, as these fluctuate with the level of business activity. Manage these costs by adjusting your operations to match demand, such as using part-time drivers during peak times.

Pricing Strategies

1. **Competitive Analysis**: Study your competitors' pricing strategies to ensure your prices are competitive. However, don't undercut your prices too much, as it may impact your profitability.
2. **Value-Based Pricing**: Consider value-based pricing, where you set prices based on the perceived value to the customer rather than just the cost. Highlight the unique benefits and superior service your business offers.
3. **Dynamic Pricing**: Implement dynamic pricing strategies that adjust prices based on demand, time of day, or delivery distance. This can help maximize revenue during peak times and attract more customers during off-peak hours.
4. **Discounts and Promotions**: Use discounts and promotions strategically to attract new customers or encourage repeat business. Ensure that these promotional activities are financially viable and do not erode your profit margins.

Financial Planning and Analysis

1. **Financial Goals**: Set clear financial goals for your business, such as revenue targets, profit margins, and cost reduction objectives. Regularly review and adjust these goals based on performance and market conditions.
2. **Profit and Loss Statement**: Maintain a detailed profit and loss statement (P&L) to track your revenue, costs, and profitability. Regularly review your P&L to identify trends, opportunities, and areas for improvement.
3. **Break-Even Analysis**: Conduct a break-even analysis to determine the minimum sales needed to cover costs. This helps you set realistic sales targets and pricing strategies.

4. **Investment Planning**: Plan for future investments, whether it's expanding your fleet, upgrading technology, or marketing initiatives. Ensure that you have the financial capacity to support these investments without compromising daily operations.

Financial Reporting and Compliance

1. **Regular Reporting**: Generate regular financial reports, such as monthly income statements, balance sheets, and cash flow statements. These reports provide insights into your business's financial health and guide strategic decisions.
2. **Tax Compliance**: Stay compliant with local tax regulations by keeping accurate financial records and filing taxes on time. Consider hiring a professional accountant to manage your tax obligations and maximize deductions.
3. **Audits and Reviews**: Conduct regular internal audits and financial reviews to ensure accuracy and integrity in your financial reporting. This helps identify discrepancies, prevent fraud, and maintain transparency.

Conclusion

Effective financial management is crucial for the sustainability and growth of your delivery business. By creating detailed budgets, managing cash flow, controlling costs, implementing strategic pricing, and conducting thorough financial analysis, you can ensure your business remains profitable and resilient. In the next chapter, we'll explore the legal aspects of running a delivery business, including regulations, contracts, and compliance requirements. Understanding the legal landscape will help you navigate potential challenges and protect your business interests.

Chapter 20: Legal Considerations for Your Delivery Business

Welcome to Chapter 20 of your journey into starting a delivery business! In this chapter, we'll cover the essential legal considerations you need to understand to operate your delivery business smoothly and lawfully. Navigating the legal landscape is crucial for protecting your business, avoiding fines, and ensuring compliance with all regulations.

Understanding Legal Structures

1. **Choosing a Business Structure**: The first step is to decide on the legal structure of your business. Common options include:
   - **Sole Proprietorship**: Simplest form, but personal assets are not protected.
   - **Partnership**: Shared ownership, but partners are personally liable.
   - **Limited Liability Company (LLC)**: Offers personal liability protection and flexible management.
   - **Corporation**: More complex, with benefits like limited liability and potential tax advantages.
2. **Registering Your Business**: Once you choose a structure, register your business with the appropriate local, state, and federal authorities. This includes obtaining an Employer Identification Number (EIN) from the IRS if you have employees or operate as a corporation or partnership.

Licensing and Permits

1. **Business Licenses**: Most areas require a general business license to operate legally. Check with your local government to understand the specific requirements for your location.
2. **Special Permits**: Depending on your services, you may need special permits. For instance, transporting goods across state lines may require federal permits from the Department of Transportation (DOT).

3. **Zoning Permits**: Ensure your business complies with local zoning laws, especially if you operate from a home office or warehouse. Some areas restrict commercial activities in residential zones.

Compliance with Transportation Laws

1. **Driver Requirements**: Ensure all drivers have valid licenses and meet any additional qualifications, such as Commercial Driver's Licenses (CDLs) for larger vehicles. Conduct regular background checks and maintain driving records.
2. **Vehicle Regulations**: Keep all vehicles registered, insured, and regularly inspected for safety compliance. Adhere to weight limits, emissions standards, and other local or federal regulations.
3. **Safety Protocols**: Implement strict safety protocols and training for drivers to reduce the risk of accidents and liability. Compliance with Occupational Safety and Health Administration (OSHA) guidelines is essential for workplace safety.

Insurance Needs

1. **General Liability Insurance**: Covers bodily injuries, property damage, and personal injury claims. Essential for protecting your business against lawsuits.
2. **Commercial Auto Insurance**: Covers your delivery vehicles. Provides protection against accidents, theft, and damage.
3. **Workers' Compensation Insurance**: Required in most states if you have employees. Covers medical expenses and lost wages for employees injured on the job.
4. **Cargo Insurance**: Protects the goods you're transporting against loss or damage. Important for maintaining trust with clients.

Contracts and Agreements

1. **Customer Contracts**: Draft clear contracts outlining the terms and conditions of your delivery services, including pricing,

delivery schedules, and liability limits. This protects both you and your clients.
2. **Employee Agreements**: Create employment contracts detailing job responsibilities, compensation, and workplace policies. Include non-compete and confidentiality clauses where appropriate.
3. **Vendor Agreements**: When working with suppliers or partners, ensure you have detailed agreements that specify terms of service, payment schedules, and performance expectations.

Intellectual Property

1. **Trademarks**: Protect your brand name, logo, and other identifying marks by registering trademarks. This prevents others from using similar branding that could confuse your customers.
2. **Copyrights**: If you create unique content for your marketing, such as blogs, videos, or promotional materials, consider copyrighting them to protect your intellectual property.

Data Privacy and Security

1. **Data Protection Laws**: Comply with data protection regulations like the General Data Protection Regulation (GDPR) if you handle personal data of customers, especially if operating internationally.
2. **Cybersecurity Measures**: Implement robust cybersecurity measures to protect sensitive information from breaches. Use encryption, secure servers, and regularly update your software.

Tax Compliance

1. **Federal Taxes**: Understand your federal tax obligations, including income tax, payroll tax, and self-employment tax. Filing quarterly estimated taxes may be necessary.

2. **State and Local Taxes**: Stay informed about state and local tax requirements, including sales tax, use tax, and business property tax. Each jurisdiction has different regulations.
3. **Tax Deductions**: Keep detailed records of business expenses to maximize tax deductions. This can include vehicle expenses, office supplies, and marketing costs.

Handling Legal Disputes

1. **Dispute Resolution**: Establish clear policies for handling disputes with customers, employees, or vendors. Consider mediation or arbitration as cost-effective alternatives to litigation.
2. **Legal Counsel**: Maintain a relationship with a business attorney who can provide legal advice, review contracts, and represent you in disputes. Proactive legal support can prevent many issues before they arise.

Staying Informed

1. **Regulatory Changes**: Laws and regulations change frequently. Stay informed through industry associations, legal newsletters, and government websites to ensure ongoing compliance.
2. **Continuous Education**: Invest in continuous education for yourself and your team. Attend workshops, webinars, and training sessions on legal and regulatory topics relevant to your business.

Conclusion

Navigating the legal landscape is a critical component of running a successful delivery business. By understanding and complying with business structures, licensing, transportation laws, insurance needs, contracts, intellectual property, data privacy, tax obligations, and dispute resolution processes, you can protect your business and ensure its long-term success. In the next chapter, we'll explore the importance of customer service and strategies to enhance your customer experience, ensuring your delivery business not only survives but thrives in a competitive market.

Chapter 21: Customer Service Excellence in Your Delivery Business

Welcome to Chapter 21 of your journey into running a successful delivery business! In this chapter, we'll explore the crucial role of customer service and how you can achieve excellence in serving your customers. Exceptional customer service is not just about delivering packages; it's about creating memorable experiences, building loyalty, and differentiating your business from competitors.

The Importance of Customer Service

1. **Customer Retention**: Providing excellent customer service fosters loyalty and encourages repeat business. Satisfied customers are more likely to choose your delivery service again and recommend it to others.
2. **Competitive Advantage**: In a competitive market, superior customer service sets your business apart. It becomes a key differentiator that attracts new customers and enhances your brand reputation.
3. **Brand Ambassadors**: Happy customers become advocates for your business, spreading positive word-of-mouth and contributing to organic growth.

Building a Customer-Centric Culture

1. **Training and Empowerment**: Train your team to prioritize customer satisfaction. Empower employees to resolve issues promptly and effectively, giving them the authority and resources to make decisions that benefit customers.
2. **Communication Skills**: Effective communication is essential. Ensure your team communicates clearly, listens actively to customer concerns, and provides empathetic responses.
3. **Consistency**: Maintain consistency in service standards across all touchpoints, whether it's in-person interactions, phone calls, emails, or social media engagement. Consistency builds trust and reliability.

Understanding Customer Expectations

1. **Know Your Customers**: Develop detailed customer profiles and understand their preferences, expectations, and pain points. Tailor your services to meet their needs effectively.
2. **Feedback Mechanisms**: Implement feedback systems such as surveys, reviews, and customer satisfaction ratings. Use this data to identify areas for improvement and gauge customer sentiment.
3. **Anticipate Needs**: Proactively anticipate customer needs based on past interactions and behaviors. Offer personalized recommendations and solutions that add value to their experience.

Key Elements of Excellent Customer Service

1. **Accessibility and Responsiveness**: Ensure customers can reach you easily through multiple channels (phone, email, chat). Respond promptly to inquiries, concerns, and delivery status updates.
2. **Transparency**: Be transparent about delivery times, pricing, and service capabilities. Set realistic expectations and provide updates if there are delays or issues.
3. **Problem Resolution**: Empower your team to resolve customer issues promptly and effectively. Implement a clear escalation process for handling complex problems.

Enhancing the Delivery Experience

1. **Timeliness**: Deliver packages on time as promised. Use technology like GPS tracking to provide customers with real-time updates on their deliveries.
2. **Security and Care**: Handle packages with care and ensure they arrive in pristine condition. Implement security measures to prevent loss or damage during transit.

3. **Contactless Options**: Offer contactless delivery options for customers who prefer minimal interaction. Provide clear instructions for safe drop-off locations.

Building Relationships

1. **Personalization**: Address customers by name and personalize interactions based on their preferences. Remember details about past orders or inquiries to make interactions more meaningful.
2. **Follow-Up**: Follow up with customers after delivery to ensure satisfaction. Thank them for their business and invite feedback on their experience.
3. **Customer Loyalty Programs**: Reward repeat customers with loyalty programs, discounts, or exclusive offers. Show appreciation for their continued support.

Leveraging Technology

1. **Customer Relationship Management (CRM)**: Use CRM software to manage customer interactions, track preferences, and maintain a history of communications. This helps in delivering personalized service.
2. **Automation**: Implement automation for routine tasks like order confirmations, delivery notifications, and customer feedback collection. Automation streamlines processes and improves efficiency.
3. **Data Analytics**: Analyze customer data to gain insights into behavior patterns, preferences, and satisfaction levels. Use this information to tailor marketing strategies and improve service delivery.

Handling Customer Complaints

1. **Listen Actively**: Listen to customer complaints without interruption. Understand their concerns fully before responding.

2. **Apologize and Resolve**: Apologize sincerely for any inconvenience caused. Resolve the issue promptly and offer compensation or solutions where appropriate.
3. **Learn and Improve**: Use customer complaints as learning opportunities. Identify root causes and implement corrective actions to prevent similar issues in the future.

Measuring Customer Satisfaction

1. **Net Promoter Score (NPS)**: Measure customer loyalty and satisfaction through NPS surveys. Ask customers how likely they are to recommend your delivery service to others.
2. **Customer Satisfaction Score (CSAT)**: Use CSAT surveys to gauge satisfaction levels after each delivery or interaction. Analyze feedback to identify areas for improvement.
3. **Feedback Analysis**: Regularly analyze customer feedback and survey results. Identify trends, common issues, and areas of strength to refine your customer service strategy.

Conclusion

Providing excellent customer service is not just a goal; it's a commitment to meeting and exceeding customer expectations at every opportunity. By building a customer-centric culture, understanding customer needs, delivering exceptional experiences, leveraging technology, and continuously improving based on feedback, you can cultivate strong customer relationships and drive business growth.

In the next chapter, we'll explore strategies for managing and optimizing your delivery fleet. Learn how to maximize efficiency, reduce costs, and ensure reliability in your delivery operations.

Chapter 22: Managing and Optimizing Your Delivery Fleet

Welcome to Chapter 22 of your journey into running a successful delivery business! In this chapter, we'll explore the essential aspects of managing and optimizing your delivery fleet. Your fleet is at the heart of your operations, and efficient management can significantly impact your business's profitability, customer satisfaction, and overall success.

Fleet Management Basics

1. **Understanding Your Fleet**: Assess the size and composition of your fleet based on the volume of deliveries, geographic coverage, and types of goods transported. Consider factors like vehicle capacity, fuel efficiency, and maintenance requirements.
2. **Fleet Tracking and Management Systems**: Implement GPS tracking and fleet management software to monitor vehicle locations, optimize routes, and improve operational efficiency. These systems provide real-time data for better decision-making.
3. **Maintenance and Upkeep**: Regularly maintain and service your vehicles to ensure they are in optimal condition. Scheduled maintenance prevents breakdowns, extends vehicle lifespan, and reduces operational disruptions.

Optimizing Delivery Routes

1. **Route Planning Tools**: Use route planning software to optimize delivery routes based on factors like distance, traffic patterns, delivery windows, and vehicle capacity. Efficient routes save time, fuel costs, and improve delivery reliability.
2. **Real-Time Adjustments**: Monitor traffic and weather conditions in real-time to make adjustments to delivery routes as needed. This proactive approach minimizes delays and ensures timely deliveries.

3. **Driver Feedback**: Encourage drivers to provide feedback on route efficiency and potential improvements. Their insights can lead to route optimizations that save time and improve overall productivity.

Vehicle Selection and Efficiency

1. **Choosing the Right Vehicles**: Select vehicles that match your delivery needs, such as vans, trucks, or specialized vehicles for fragile or perishable goods. Consider factors like fuel efficiency, payload capacity, and environmental impact.
2. **Fuel Efficiency**: Promote fuel-efficient driving habits among your drivers, such as reducing idling time, maintaining steady speeds, and avoiding aggressive acceleration and braking. This helps reduce fuel costs and carbon emissions.
3. **Alternative Fuels and Technologies**: Explore options for alternative fuels (electric, hybrid) and technologies (telematics, autonomous vehicles) that can further improve fuel efficiency and sustainability in your fleet.

Driver Management and Training

1. **Driver Safety**: Prioritize driver safety through rigorous training programs and adherence to safety protocols. Educate drivers on defensive driving techniques, handling hazardous materials, and emergency procedures.
2. **Driver Monitoring**: Monitor driver behavior and performance using telematics and GPS tracking systems. Track metrics like speeding, harsh braking, and route adherence to identify areas for improvement and ensure compliance with regulations.
3. **Performance Incentives**: Implement performance incentives based on safe driving practices, on-time deliveries, and customer satisfaction metrics. Recognizing and rewarding top-performing drivers boosts morale and enhances productivity.

Inventory Management

1. **Inventory Tracking**: Use inventory management software to track goods from warehouse to delivery. Maintain accurate inventory records to prevent stockouts, manage perishable items effectively, and fulfill customer orders efficiently.
2. **Cross-Docking**: Implement cross-docking strategies to streamline the transfer of goods from inbound to outbound vehicles without storing them in warehouses. This reduces handling costs and shortens delivery times.
3. **Just-in-Time Delivery**: Adopt just-in-time delivery practices to minimize inventory holding costs. Coordinate deliveries closely with production schedules to ensure goods arrive precisely when needed.

Technology Integration

1. **Fleet Telematics**: Utilize telematics systems to gather and analyze data on vehicle performance, driver behavior, and route efficiency. Use insights to optimize operations, reduce costs, and improve service quality.
2. **Internet of Things (IoT)**: Implement IoT sensors to monitor vehicle conditions (temperature, humidity) and cargo status in real-time. This ensures goods are delivered in optimal conditions and enhances customer satisfaction.
3. **Blockchain Technology**: Explore blockchain for transparent and secure supply chain management. Blockchain can track product provenance, verify delivery authenticity, and streamline payment processes.

Environmental Sustainability

1. **Green Fleet Initiatives**: Implement eco-friendly practices such as vehicle electrification, idle reduction technologies, and route optimization for reduced carbon emissions. Committing to sustainability can attract environmentally conscious customers and reduce operational costs.
2. **Emission Reduction Strategies**: Comply with environmental regulations and adopt emission reduction strategies. Invest in

vehicles with low emissions or retrofit existing vehicles with eco-friendly technologies.
3. **Corporate Social Responsibility (CSR)**: Engage in CSR initiatives focused on environmental stewardship and community involvement. Communicate your commitment to sustainability to customers and stakeholders.

Performance Monitoring and Metrics

1. **Key Performance Indicators (KPIs)**: Track KPIs such as on-time delivery rates, fuel efficiency, vehicle utilization, and driver productivity. Regularly analyze performance metrics to identify trends, strengths, and areas for improvement.
2. **Benchmarking**: Benchmark your fleet performance against industry standards and competitors. Identify best practices and implement continuous improvements to maintain a competitive edge.
3. **Data-Driven Decision Making**: Use data analytics to make informed decisions about fleet operations, resource allocation, and strategic planning. Leverage predictive analytics to anticipate trends and optimize future performance.

Conclusion

Effective management and optimization of your delivery fleet are critical for achieving operational efficiency, reducing costs, and delivering exceptional customer experiences. By focusing on route optimization, vehicle efficiency, driver management, technology integration, sustainability initiatives, and performance monitoring, you can streamline operations and position your delivery business for sustainable growth.

In the next chapter, we'll explore innovative technologies transforming the delivery industry. Learn about drones, autonomous vehicles, and other advancements shaping the future of logistics and delivery services.

Chapter 23: Marketing Strategies for Your Delivery Business

Welcome to Chapter 23 of your journey into running a successful delivery business! In this chapter, we will explore effective marketing strategies tailored specifically for your delivery service. Marketing plays a crucial role in attracting customers, building brand awareness, and differentiating your business in a competitive market. Let's dive into the strategies and tactics that will help you reach your target audience and grow your delivery business.

Understanding Your Target Audience

1. **Market Segmentation**: Identify and segment your target audience based on demographics (age, gender, income), psychographics (lifestyles, values), and geographic location. Understanding your audience allows you to tailor your marketing efforts effectively.
2. **Customer Persona Development**: Create detailed customer personas that represent your ideal customers. Include information such as their needs, preferences, pain points, and buying behavior. This helps in crafting personalized marketing messages.
3. **Competitive Analysis**: Conduct a competitive analysis to understand your competitors' strengths, weaknesses, pricing strategies, and marketing tactics. Differentiate your delivery service by highlighting unique features and benefits.

Developing Your Marketing Strategy

1. **Clear Value Proposition**: Define a clear value proposition that communicates the unique benefits of choosing your delivery service. Highlight factors such as reliability, speed, affordability, and customer service excellence.
2. **Branding**: Develop a strong brand identity that resonates with your target audience. Create a memorable logo, color scheme, and brand voice that reflects your business values and appeals to customers.

3. **Integrated Marketing Approach**: Implement an integrated marketing approach that combines online and offline channels to reach customers effectively. This may include digital marketing, social media, content marketing, email campaigns, and traditional advertising.

Online Marketing Strategies

1. **Website Optimization**: Create a user-friendly website that showcases your delivery services, pricing, service areas, and customer testimonials. Optimize the website for search engines (SEO) to improve visibility and attract organic traffic.
2. **Search Engine Marketing (SEM)**: Launch paid search campaigns (Google Ads) to target customers searching for delivery services online. Use targeted keywords related to your business to drive relevant traffic to your website.
3. **Content Marketing**: Produce valuable content such as blogs, articles, and guides related to delivery tips, industry trends, and customer success stories. Content marketing establishes your expertise and attracts potential customers.
4. **Social Media Marketing**: Leverage social media platforms (Facebook, Instagram, LinkedIn) to engage with your audience, share updates, promote special offers, and showcase customer testimonials. Use targeted advertising to reach specific demographics.

Customer Referral Programs

1. **Incentivize Referrals**: Implement a customer referral program that rewards existing customers for referring new clients to your delivery service. Offer discounts, credits, or free deliveries as incentives for successful referrals.
2. **Word-of-Mouth Marketing**: Encourage satisfied customers to share their positive experiences with friends, family, and colleagues. Provide exceptional service and exceed customer expectations to stimulate word-of-mouth promotion.

Email Marketing Campaigns

1. **Build an Email List**: Collect email addresses from customers and prospects through website sign-ups, promotions, and delivery transactions. Segment your email list based on customer preferences and behaviors.
2. **Personalized Campaigns**: Send personalized email campaigns that deliver relevant content, special offers, and updates tailored to each segment of your audience. Use automation tools to schedule and track email performance.

Community Engagement and Partnerships

1. **Local Partnerships**: Collaborate with local businesses, restaurants, e-commerce platforms, and event organizers to offer delivery services. Establish mutually beneficial partnerships that expand your customer base and enhance brand visibility.
2. **Community Involvement**: Participate in community events, sponsor local initiatives, and support charitable causes. Community involvement builds goodwill, fosters brand loyalty, and strengthens your reputation as a responsible business.

Customer Feedback and Reviews

1. **Monitor Reviews**: Monitor online reviews and customer feedback on platforms like Google My Business, Yelp, and social media. Respond promptly to both positive and negative reviews to demonstrate responsiveness and commitment to customer satisfaction.
2. **Use Customer Feedback**: Use feedback to improve service quality, address customer concerns, and refine your marketing strategy. Positive reviews can serve as testimonials that attract new customers.

Measurement and Optimization

1. **Track Key Metrics**: Measure the effectiveness of your marketing campaigns by tracking key metrics such as website traffic, conversion rates, customer acquisition cost (CAC), and return on investment (ROI). Use analytics tools to gain insights into campaign performance.
2. **Continuous Optimization**: Continuously optimize your marketing efforts based on data-driven insights and performance metrics. Experiment with different strategies, A/B test campaigns, and refine your approach to maximize results.

Conclusion

Implementing effective marketing strategies is essential for growing your delivery business and attracting new customers. By understanding your target audience, developing a clear value proposition, leveraging online and offline channels, fostering customer relationships, and continuously optimizing your marketing efforts, you can differentiate your delivery service and achieve sustainable growth.

In the next chapter, we'll explore customer retention strategies to cultivate long-term relationships with your clients. Learn how to enhance customer loyalty, reduce churn, and turn first-time customers into loyal advocates for your delivery business.

Chapter 24: Customer Retention Strategies for Your Delivery Business

Welcome to Chapter 24 of your journey into running a successful delivery business! In this chapter, we will focus on customer retention strategies. Retaining customers is just as important, if not more so, than acquiring new ones. Loyal customers not only provide repeat business but also become brand advocates, spreading the word about your excellent service. Let's delve into practical and effective ways to keep your customers coming back.

Understanding the Importance of Customer Retention

1. **Cost Efficiency**: Acquiring new customers can be five times more expensive than retaining existing ones. By focusing on customer retention, you save on marketing and sales expenses.
2. **Increased Profits**: Repeat customers are likely to spend more and more frequently than new customers. This leads to higher average order values and increased revenue over time.
3. **Brand Loyalty**: Loyal customers are more forgiving of occasional mistakes and are less likely to switch to competitors. They also provide valuable feedback to help you improve your service.

Building Strong Customer Relationships

1. **Personalized Communication**: Use customer data to personalize communication. Address customers by their names and send personalized messages based on their preferences and past interactions.
2. **Regular Engagement**: Stay in touch with your customers through regular emails, newsletters, and social media updates. Keep them informed about new services, special offers, and company news.
3. **Customer Appreciation**: Show appreciation to your customers through thank-you notes, special discounts, and loyalty rewards. Recognize and celebrate customer milestones, such as anniversaries of their first delivery.

Providing Exceptional Customer Service

1. **Responsive Support**: Ensure that your customer service team is easily accessible and responsive. Quick resolution of issues and queries enhances customer satisfaction and loyalty.
2. **Proactive Service**: Anticipate customer needs and address potential issues before they arise. For example, notify customers about possible delivery delays and offer solutions proactively.
3. **Exceeding Expectations**: Go the extra mile to exceed customer expectations. Small gestures like handwritten thank-you notes or a follow-up call to ensure satisfaction can make a big difference.

Implementing Loyalty Programs

1. **Reward Systems**: Create a loyalty program that rewards customers for their repeat business. Offer points for every delivery, which can be redeemed for discounts, free services, or exclusive offers.
2. **Referral Incentives**: Encourage existing customers to refer new customers by offering incentives such as discounts or freebies for successful referrals.
3. **Exclusive Benefits**: Provide loyal customers with exclusive benefits such as priority delivery, special discounts, or access to new services before they are available to the general public.

Leveraging Technology for Retention

1. **Customer Relationship Management (CRM)**: Use CRM software to keep track of customer interactions, preferences, and feedback. This helps in providing personalized service and identifying opportunities for engagement.
2. **Automation Tools**: Utilize automation tools to send personalized emails, reminders, and follow-ups. Automation ensures consistent communication and saves time.

3. **Data Analytics**: Analyze customer data to understand behavior patterns, preferences, and trends. Use these insights to tailor your services and marketing efforts to meet customer needs better.

Creating a Seamless Delivery Experience

1. **Reliable and Timely Deliveries**: Ensure that deliveries are always reliable and on time. Consistency in service builds trust and encourages repeat business.
2. **Transparent Tracking**: Provide customers with real-time tracking of their deliveries. Transparency in the delivery process enhances trust and satisfaction.
3. **Flexible Options**: Offer flexible delivery options such as same-day delivery, scheduled deliveries, and convenient return policies. Flexibility caters to different customer needs and preferences.

Gathering and Utilizing Customer Feedback

1. **Feedback Channels**: Create multiple channels for customers to provide feedback, such as surveys, reviews, and direct contact options. Make it easy for them to share their opinions.
2. **Acting on Feedback**: Show customers that their feedback is valued by acting on it. Implement changes based on their suggestions and communicate the improvements made.
3. **Closing the Loop**: Follow up with customers who have provided feedback to inform them of the actions taken. This demonstrates that you listen and care about their input.

Building a Community

1. **Social Media Engagement**: Use social media platforms to engage with your customers, share updates, and create a sense of community. Encourage customers to share their experiences and participate in discussions.

2. **Events and Webinars**: Host events, webinars, or live Q&A sessions to connect with your customers and provide valuable information. These interactions build stronger relationships.
3. **Customer Stories**: Share customer success stories and testimonials on your website and social media. Highlighting real experiences builds trust and showcases the value of your service.

Monitoring Retention Metrics

1. **Customer Retention Rate**: Track your customer retention rate to understand the percentage of customers who continue to use your services over a specific period. This metric helps gauge the effectiveness of your retention strategies.
2. **Customer Lifetime Value (CLV)**: Calculate the average revenue generated from a customer over their lifetime. Increasing CLV indicates successful retention efforts.
3. **Churn Rate**: Monitor your churn rate to understand the percentage of customers who stop using your services. Identifying reasons for churn helps in addressing issues and improving retention.

Conclusion

Customer retention is vital for the long-term success of your delivery business. By building strong relationships, providing exceptional service, implementing loyalty programs, leveraging technology, and continuously improving based on feedback, you can foster customer loyalty and drive sustained growth. In the next chapter, we'll explore advanced financial management strategies to ensure your delivery business remains profitable and financially healthy.

Chapter 25: Advanced Financial Management for Your Delivery Business

Welcome to Chapter 25 of your journey into running a successful delivery business! This chapter delves into advanced financial management strategies to ensure your delivery business remains profitable, sustainable, and ready for growth. Understanding and effectively managing your finances is crucial for making informed decisions, securing funding, and maximizing your bottom line. Let's explore key financial management practices that will set your business up for long-term success.

Setting Financial Goals

1. **Short-Term and Long-Term Goals**: Establish clear financial goals for both the short-term (monthly, quarterly) and long-term (annually, multi-year). These goals should be specific, measurable, achievable, relevant, and time-bound (SMART).
2. **Budgeting**: Develop a detailed budget that outlines your expected revenues, fixed and variable costs, and capital expenditures. Regularly review and adjust your budget to reflect actual performance and changing circumstances.
3. **Cash Flow Projections**: Create cash flow projections to anticipate future cash needs and ensure you have sufficient liquidity to cover operational expenses. This helps prevent cash flow shortages and allows for timely financial planning.

Monitoring Financial Performance

1. **Key Financial Metrics**: Track key financial metrics such as gross profit margin, net profit margin, operating expenses, and return on investment (ROI). These metrics provide insights into your business's financial health and performance.
2. **Financial Statements**: Regularly review your financial statements, including the income statement, balance sheet, and cash flow statement. These documents offer a comprehensive

view of your financial position and help identify trends and areas for improvement.
3. **Variance Analysis**: Perform variance analysis to compare actual financial performance against your budget and projections. Identify significant deviations and investigate their causes to take corrective actions.

Cost Management

1. **Fixed and Variable Costs**: Distinguish between fixed costs (rent, salaries) and variable costs (fuel, maintenance). Understanding these costs helps in better managing your expenses and improving profitability.
2. **Cost Control Measures**: Implement cost control measures such as negotiating with suppliers, optimizing delivery routes, and reducing waste. Regularly review expenses to identify cost-saving opportunities.
3. **Break-Even Analysis**: Conduct break-even analysis to determine the sales volume needed to cover your costs. This analysis helps in setting pricing strategies and assessing the impact of cost changes on profitability.

Pricing Strategies

1. **Competitive Pricing**: Research your competitors' pricing to ensure your rates are competitive while still covering costs and generating profit. Consider factors such as service quality, delivery speed, and value-added services.
2. **Dynamic Pricing**: Implement dynamic pricing strategies that adjust rates based on demand, delivery times, and distance. This approach can maximize revenue during peak periods and attract more customers during off-peak times.
3. **Discounts and Promotions**: Offer discounts and promotions to attract new customers and encourage repeat business. Ensure these incentives are financially viable and do not erode your profit margins.

Funding and Investment

1. **Self-Funding**: Assess your personal financial resources and consider self-funding options to start or expand your business. This includes savings, personal loans, and contributions from friends and family.
2. **External Funding**: Explore external funding options such as bank loans, venture capital, and angel investors. Prepare a compelling business plan and financial projections to present to potential investors or lenders.
3. **Reinvestment**: Allocate a portion of your profits for reinvestment into the business. Reinvesting in areas such as technology, equipment, and marketing can drive growth and improve operational efficiency.

Risk Management

1. **Insurance Coverage**: Ensure adequate insurance coverage to protect your business from potential risks such as accidents, theft, liability, and property damage. Review and update your policies regularly.
2. **Contingency Planning**: Develop contingency plans to address potential financial challenges such as economic downturns, cash flow shortages, and unexpected expenses. Having a plan in place helps you respond effectively to crises.
3. **Diversification**: Diversify your revenue streams by offering additional services such as warehousing, packaging, or specialized delivery options. Diversification reduces dependence on a single revenue source and mitigates risks.

Tax Planning and Compliance

1. **Tax Obligations**: Understand your tax obligations and ensure timely payment of taxes. This includes income tax, sales tax, payroll tax, and any other applicable taxes.
2. **Tax Deductions and Credits**: Identify and take advantage of tax deductions and credits available to your business. This may

include deductions for business expenses, depreciation, and incentives for specific investments.
3. **Professional Advice**: Consult with a tax advisor or accountant to ensure compliance with tax regulations and optimize your tax strategy. Professional advice can help you avoid penalties and maximize tax savings.

Financial Technology and Tools

1. **Accounting Software**: Utilize accounting software to streamline financial management tasks such as invoicing, expense tracking, and financial reporting. Popular options include QuickBooks, Xero, and FreshBooks.
2. **Financial Dashboards**: Implement financial dashboards to monitor key metrics and performance indicators in real-time. Dashboards provide a visual representation of your financial data and aid in decision-making.
3. **Automated Payments**: Set up automated payment systems for recurring expenses such as rent, utilities, and payroll. Automation reduces administrative workload and ensures timely payments.

Continuous Improvement

1. **Financial Reviews**: Conduct regular financial reviews to assess your business's performance, identify trends, and make data-driven decisions. Reviews should involve key stakeholders and financial advisors.
2. **Training and Education**: Invest in financial literacy and training for yourself and your team. Understanding financial principles and best practices enhances your ability to manage and grow your business effectively.
3. **Adapting to Changes**: Stay informed about industry trends, economic conditions, and regulatory changes that may impact your business. Adapt your financial strategies accordingly to stay competitive and resilient.

Conclusion

Advanced financial management is essential for the sustainability and growth of your delivery business. By setting clear financial goals, monitoring performance, managing costs, implementing effective pricing strategies, securing funding, and leveraging technology, you can ensure your business remains profitable and financially healthy. In the next chapter, we will explore innovative technologies transforming the delivery industry, including drones, autonomous vehicles, and other advancements shaping the future of logistics and delivery services.

Chapter 26: Embracing Technological Innovations in the Delivery Industry

Welcome to Chapter 26 of your journey into running a successful delivery business! In this chapter, we will explore the cutting-edge technological innovations transforming the delivery industry. From drones and autonomous vehicles to advanced logistics software, these innovations can streamline your operations, reduce costs, and enhance customer satisfaction. Let's dive into how you can embrace these technologies to stay ahead of the competition and future-proof your business.

The Role of Technology in Delivery Services

1. **Efficiency and Speed**: Technology can significantly improve the efficiency and speed of delivery services. Automated systems and advanced logistics software optimize routes, reduce delivery times, and increase the number of deliveries per day.
2. **Customer Satisfaction**: Modern customers expect fast, reliable, and transparent delivery services. Technological innovations provide real-time tracking, accurate delivery estimates, and seamless communication, enhancing the overall customer experience.
3. **Cost Reduction**: By automating processes and optimizing resources, technology helps reduce operational costs. This includes savings on fuel, labor, and maintenance, ultimately improving your bottom line.

Drones and Aerial Delivery Systems

1. **Drone Deliveries**: Drones are increasingly being used for last-mile deliveries, especially in hard-to-reach areas. They offer quick, efficient delivery with minimal environmental impact. While regulatory hurdles remain, many companies are successfully piloting drone delivery programs.
2. **Applications**: Drones are particularly useful for delivering small packages, medical supplies, and urgent documents. They can

bypass traffic and reach remote locations faster than traditional vehicles.
3. **Implementation**: To implement drone deliveries, invest in reliable drone technology, train your staff, and ensure compliance with local regulations. Partnering with drone delivery startups can also help you get started without a significant initial investment.

Autonomous Vehicles

1. **Self-Driving Trucks**: Autonomous trucks are being developed to transport goods over long distances. These vehicles reduce the need for human drivers, lower labor costs, and operate continuously without fatigue.
2. **Last-Mile Robots**: Small, autonomous delivery robots are being used for last-mile deliveries in urban areas. They navigate sidewalks and deliver packages directly to customers' doorsteps.
3. **Benefits**: Autonomous vehicles enhance safety, reduce delivery times, and lower operational costs. They also enable 24/7 deliveries, improving service availability and customer convenience.
4. **Challenges**: While promising, autonomous vehicle technology is still evolving. Considerations include regulatory compliance, public acceptance, and technological reliability.

Advanced Logistics Software

1. **Route Optimization**: Modern logistics software uses algorithms to optimize delivery routes, reducing fuel consumption and delivery times. It considers factors like traffic conditions, delivery windows, and vehicle capacity.
2. **Inventory Management**: Integrated inventory management systems provide real-time visibility into stock levels, helping you manage orders efficiently and reduce out-of-stock situations.
3. **Fleet Management**: Fleet management software tracks vehicle performance, maintenance schedules, and driver behavior. This

helps in reducing downtime, ensuring vehicle health, and improving overall fleet efficiency.

Real-Time Tracking and Communication

1. **GPS Tracking**: GPS tracking systems provide real-time location data of your delivery vehicles. This allows customers to track their orders and gives you visibility into fleet movements.
2. **Customer Notifications**: Automated notifications keep customers informed about their delivery status, estimated arrival times, and any delays. This transparency enhances trust and satisfaction.
3. **Driver Communication**: Equip your drivers with mobile devices or communication tools to receive route updates, traffic alerts, and customer instructions in real-time.

Artificial Intelligence and Machine Learning

1. **Demand Forecasting**: AI and machine learning algorithms analyze historical data to predict demand patterns. This helps in optimizing inventory levels, staffing, and delivery schedules.
2. **Customer Insights**: AI can analyze customer behavior and preferences to provide personalized recommendations, targeted marketing, and improved customer service.
3. **Predictive Maintenance**: Machine learning models predict when vehicles are likely to require maintenance, preventing breakdowns and reducing repair costs.

Blockchain and Secure Transactions

1. **Supply Chain Transparency**: Blockchain technology ensures transparency and traceability in the supply chain. It records every transaction, from production to delivery, in a secure, immutable ledger.
2. **Payment Security**: Blockchain enhances payment security by encrypting transactions and reducing fraud risks. It also enables faster, more efficient cross-border payments.

3. **Smart Contracts**: Smart contracts automatically execute agreements when predefined conditions are met, reducing the need for intermediaries and speeding up processes.

Environmental Sustainability

1. **Electric Vehicles**: Transitioning to electric delivery vehicles reduces your carbon footprint and operational costs. Many cities offer incentives for businesses adopting electric vehicles.
2. **Eco-Friendly Packaging**: Use biodegradable and recyclable packaging materials to minimize environmental impact. Customers increasingly prefer businesses that prioritize sustainability.
3. **Route Efficiency**: Optimizing delivery routes reduces fuel consumption and emissions, contributing to environmental sustainability.

Adopting Technological Innovations

1. **Assess Needs**: Identify the specific needs of your delivery business and prioritize technologies that address these needs effectively.
2. **Research and Partnerships**: Stay informed about the latest technological advancements and consider partnering with tech startups or established companies to implement new solutions.
3. **Training and Adaptation**: Invest in training your staff to use new technologies effectively. Encourage a culture of innovation and adaptability within your organization.
4. **Pilot Programs**: Start with pilot programs to test new technologies on a small scale. Evaluate their impact and scalability before full-scale implementation.

Conclusion

Embracing technological innovations is crucial for staying competitive and efficient in the evolving delivery industry. By adopting drones, autonomous vehicles, advanced logistics software, and other cutting-edge technologies, you can enhance service quality, reduce costs, and meet the growing expectations of modern customers. In the next chapter, we'll explore strategies for expanding your delivery business, including entering new markets, diversifying services, and scaling operations for sustained growth.

Chapter 27: Scaling Your Delivery Business for Growth

Welcome to Chapter 27 of your journey into running a successful delivery business! In this chapter, we will explore strategies for scaling your delivery business to achieve sustained growth and expand your market presence. Scaling involves increasing your business's capacity to handle more customers, orders, and geographic areas while maintaining or improving efficiency and profitability. Let's dive into the key steps and considerations for scaling your delivery business effectively.

Assessing Your Readiness to Scale

1. **Evaluate Current Operations**: Conduct a thorough assessment of your current operations, infrastructure, and capabilities. Determine if your business can handle increased demand without compromising on service quality or operational efficiency.
2. **Financial Stability**: Ensure your business is financially stable and has sufficient capital to support expansion efforts. Consider factors such as cash flow, profitability, and access to additional funding if needed.
3. **Market Demand**: Analyze market demand and customer feedback to identify opportunities for growth. Evaluate whether there is sufficient demand for your delivery services in new geographic areas or customer segments.

Strategies for Scaling Your Delivery Business

1. **Expand Service Offerings**: Diversify your service offerings to attract a broader customer base. Consider adding new delivery options such as same-day delivery, scheduled deliveries, or specialized delivery services for specific industries.
2. **Enter New Markets**: Identify and enter new geographic markets where there is demand for delivery services. Conduct market research to understand local preferences, competition, and regulatory requirements.

3. **Partner with Businesses**: Collaborate with e-commerce platforms, retail stores, restaurants, and other businesses to offer delivery services. Partnerships can help expand your customer reach and generate additional revenue streams.

Optimizing Operational Efficiency

1. **Streamline Processes**: Streamline your delivery processes to improve efficiency and reduce costs. Use advanced logistics software for route optimization, inventory management, and real-time tracking of deliveries.
2. **Automation and Technology**: Embrace automation and technology to automate repetitive tasks, such as order processing and vehicle dispatching. This frees up resources and allows your team to focus on strategic initiatives.
3. **Scalable Infrastructure**: Invest in scalable infrastructure, including vehicles, warehouses, and IT systems, to accommodate growth. Plan for future capacity needs and scalability when expanding operations.

Building a Reliable Team

1. **Recruit and Train**: Hire talented individuals who are passionate about customer service and logistics. Provide comprehensive training to ensure they understand your business values and service standards.
2. **Empower Your Team**: Empower your team with the tools and authority they need to make decisions and resolve issues quickly. Foster a culture of accountability, collaboration, and continuous improvement.
3. **Leadership and Delegation**: Delegate responsibilities to capable leaders within your organization. Effective delegation allows you to focus on strategic decision-making and growth initiatives.

Customer Relationship Management

1. **Enhance Customer Experience**: Prioritize customer satisfaction by delivering exceptional service at every touchpoint. Use customer feedback to continuously improve service quality and address pain points.
2. **Personalized Service**: Offer personalized service and communication tailored to each customer's preferences. Build strong relationships based on trust, reliability, and responsiveness.
3. **Feedback and Adaptation**: Encourage customer feedback and adapt your services based on their needs and expectations. Use data analytics to gain insights into customer behavior and preferences.

Financial Management and Planning

1. **Financial Forecasting**: Develop financial forecasts and projections to plan for future expenses, revenue growth, and profitability. Monitor key financial metrics to ensure financial health and sustainability.
2. **Cost Management**: Implement cost management strategies to control expenses and improve profitability. Regularly review and optimize costs related to labor, fuel, maintenance, and overhead.
3. **Investment in Growth**: Allocate resources and capital towards initiatives that support growth, such as marketing campaigns, technology upgrades, and expanding your delivery fleet.

Marketing and Branding

1. **Market Expansion Strategies**: Develop targeted marketing campaigns to promote your services in new markets and customer segments. Highlight your competitive advantages and unique value proposition.
2. **Brand Awareness**: Build brand awareness through digital marketing, social media engagement, and local advertising. Position your delivery business as a reliable and trusted partner in logistics solutions.

3. **Customer Acquisition**: Implement customer acquisition strategies to attract new customers and increase market share. Offer incentives, promotions, and referral programs to incentivize new customer sign-ups.

Scaling Responsibly

1. **Monitor Performance Metrics**: Track key performance indicators (KPIs) to measure the success of your scaling efforts. Monitor metrics such as customer acquisition cost (CAC), customer retention rate, and revenue growth.
2. **Adaptation to Challenges**: Anticipate and address challenges that arise during the scaling process, such as logistics complexities, regulatory compliance, and competitive pressures.
3. **Continuous Improvement**: Continuously iterate and improve your scaling strategies based on feedback, data analytics, and market trends. Stay agile and adaptable to changes in the business environment.

Conclusion

Scaling your delivery business requires careful planning, strategic decision-making, and a commitment to operational excellence. By expanding service offerings, entering new markets, optimizing efficiency, building a strong team, enhancing customer relationships, and maintaining financial discipline, you can achieve sustainable growth and solidify your position in the competitive delivery industry. In the next chapter, we will explore innovation in customer service and technology, focusing on enhancing the delivery experience through advanced solutions and customer-centric strategies.

Chapter 28: Enhancing Customer Experience in Your Delivery Business

Welcome to Chapter 28 of your journey in running a successful delivery business! In this chapter, we will explore how you can enhance customer experience to build loyalty, satisfaction, and trust. Providing exceptional customer service is crucial in the competitive landscape of delivery services. By focusing on the customer journey from order placement to delivery, you can differentiate your business and create long-lasting relationships with your customers.

Understanding Customer Expectations

1. **Customer-Centric Approach**: Adopt a customer-centric approach where every decision and interaction prioritizes the customer's needs and preferences. Understand what matters most to your customers, whether it's speed, reliability, or personalized service.
2. **Communication**: Clear and timely communication is key to managing customer expectations. Provide updates on order status, delivery times, and any delays to keep customers informed and reassured.
3. **Feedback Loop**: Establish a feedback loop to gather insights from your customers. Encourage reviews, surveys, and direct feedback to understand their experiences and identify areas for improvement.

Seamless Ordering Process

1. **User-Friendly Platform**: Ensure your online platform or mobile app is intuitive and user-friendly. Simplify the ordering process with clear instructions, easy navigation, and a seamless checkout experience.
2. **Transparent Pricing**: Clearly display pricing, fees, and any additional charges upfront. Avoid surprises at checkout to build trust and confidence in your pricing structure.
3. **Customization Options**: Offer customization options such as delivery time slots, package tracking, and delivery instructions.

Empower customers to tailor their delivery experience to their preferences.

Reliable and Timely Deliveries

1. **On-Time Performance**: Consistently meet or exceed promised delivery times. Use route optimization software and real-time tracking to minimize delays and optimize delivery routes.
2. **Real-Time Tracking**: Provide customers with real-time tracking of their deliveries. Transparency in the delivery process builds trust and reduces anxiety about the status of their orders.
3. **Proactive Communication**: Anticipate potential issues and communicate proactively with customers. Notify them of any delays, changes in delivery schedules, or unexpected circumstances.

Personalized Customer Service

1. **Personalization**: Address customers by name and personalize communications based on their purchase history and preferences. Show that you value their business by remembering their preferences and previous interactions.
2. **Responsive Support**: Offer responsive customer support through multiple channels such as phone, email, and live chat. Ensure that customers can easily reach a knowledgeable representative to resolve issues or answer questions.
3. **Follow-Up**: Follow up with customers after delivery to ensure satisfaction. A simple thank-you message or feedback request shows appreciation and demonstrates your commitment to customer service.

Building Trust and Reliability

1. **Reliable Service**: Consistency is key to building trust. Deliver on your promises and exceed customer expectations whenever possible. Reliability fosters loyalty and encourages repeat business.

2. **Transparency**: Be transparent about your policies, delivery processes, and service capabilities. Clearly communicate terms and conditions, return policies, and any limitations upfront.
3. **Handling Complaints**: Handle customer complaints and issues with empathy and urgency. Resolve problems promptly, offer solutions, and compensate for any inconvenience caused.

Continuous Improvement

1. **Feedback Implementation**: Act on customer feedback to continuously improve your services. Use feedback to identify trends, address recurring issues, and implement changes that enhance the customer experience.
2. **Training and Development**: Invest in training your staff to deliver exceptional customer service. Equip them with the skills and knowledge to handle customer interactions effectively and professionally.
3. **Innovation and Adaptation**: Stay ahead of customer expectations by embracing innovation and adopting new technologies. Monitor industry trends and implement solutions that enhance efficiency and convenience for your customers.

Loyalty Programs and Incentives

1. **Rewards and Discounts**: Implement loyalty programs that reward customers for repeat business. Offer incentives such as discounts, free deliveries, or exclusive offers for loyal customers.
2. **Referral Programs**: Encourage satisfied customers to refer friends and family by offering incentives for successful referrals. Word-of-mouth recommendations are powerful for acquiring new customers.
3. **Exclusive Benefits**: Provide loyal customers with exclusive benefits such as priority scheduling, early access to promotions, or personalized offers based on their purchase history.

Community Engagement and Brand Advocacy

1. **Social Responsibility**: Engage with your local community through sponsorships, charitable donations, or environmentally friendly practices. Show that your business is committed to making a positive impact.
2. **Customer Advocacy**: Cultivate brand advocates by delivering exceptional experiences that customers are eager to share. Encourage satisfied customers to leave reviews and testimonials that attract new business.
3. **Partnerships and Collaborations**: Collaborate with other businesses or influencers to extend your reach and attract new customers. Partnering with complementary brands can create mutually beneficial opportunities.

Conclusion

Enhancing customer experience is not just about delivering packages—it's about building relationships based on trust, reliability, and exceptional service. By focusing on understanding and meeting customer expectations, providing seamless ordering and delivery processes, offering personalized service, and continuously improving based on feedback, you can differentiate your delivery business in a competitive market. In the next chapter, we will explore the future of delivery logistics, including emerging trends and technologies shaping the industry's evolution.

Chapter 29: The Future of Delivery Logistics: Emerging Trends and Technologies

Welcome to Chapter 29 of your journey in the world of delivery logistics! In this chapter, we'll explore the exciting developments and innovations shaping the future of the delivery industry. From advanced technologies to evolving consumer expectations, understanding these trends will help you stay ahead and adapt your business for sustained success.

Technological Advancements in Delivery Logistics

1. **Autonomous Vehicles**: The rise of autonomous vehicles, including self-driving trucks and delivery drones, is revolutionizing logistics. These vehicles can operate 24/7, reduce delivery times, and lower operational costs by eliminating the need for human drivers.
2. **Drone Deliveries**: Drones are increasingly used for last-mile deliveries, especially in urban areas. They can navigate congested traffic and deliver packages swiftly, enhancing efficiency and customer satisfaction.
3. **Robotics in Warehousing**: Automated robots are transforming warehouse operations. They streamline picking, packing, and sorting processes, reducing errors and accelerating order fulfillment.

Sustainable and Eco-Friendly Practices

1. **Electric Vehicles (EVs)**: The shift towards electric delivery vehicles is reducing carbon emissions and operational costs. Governments and businesses are incentivizing EV adoption to promote environmental sustainability.
2. **Green Packaging Solutions**: Eco-friendly packaging materials, such as biodegradable plastics and recycled materials, are gaining popularity. They minimize environmental impact and appeal to environmentally conscious consumers.

3. **Route Optimization for Efficiency**: Advanced algorithms optimize delivery routes to minimize fuel consumption and reduce carbon footprint. Real-time data and predictive analytics further enhance route efficiency.

Enhanced Customer Experience

1. **Real-Time Tracking and Transparency**: Customers expect real-time updates on their deliveries. Enhanced tracking technologies provide accurate delivery estimates and notifications, improving transparency and trust.
2. **Personalized Delivery Options**: Customizable delivery preferences, such as delivery time slots and secure drop-off locations, cater to individual customer needs. Personalization enhances convenience and satisfaction.
3. **Instant Delivery Services**: The demand for instant gratification has led to the popularity of same-day and on-demand delivery services. Businesses are investing in infrastructure and partnerships to meet this demand.

Data Analytics and Predictive Insights

1. **Demand Forecasting**: AI-driven analytics predict demand patterns based on historical data and market trends. Accurate forecasting enables businesses to optimize inventory management and resource allocation.
2. **Predictive Maintenance**: IoT sensors monitor vehicle performance and predict maintenance needs before breakdowns occur. Proactive maintenance minimizes downtime and enhances fleet reliability.
3. **Customer Behavior Analysis**: Analyzing customer behavior and preferences helps businesses tailor services and marketing strategies. Data-driven insights foster customer loyalty and drive business growth.

Blockchain Technology in Supply Chain Management

1. **Transparent Supply Chains**: Blockchain technology enhances transparency and traceability throughout the supply chain. It securely records transactions, from production to delivery, reducing fraud and improving accountability.
2. **Smart Contracts**: Smart contracts automate and enforce contract terms between parties. They streamline transactions, eliminate intermediaries, and ensure compliance with agreed-upon conditions.
3. **Secure Payments**: Blockchain-based payment systems provide secure and efficient transactions. They facilitate faster cross-border payments and reduce transaction costs for businesses and consumers.

Agility and Adaptability in Operations

1. **Flexible Delivery Models**: Businesses are adopting flexible delivery models to meet diverse customer needs. Options like click-and-collect, subscription services, and crowd-sourced delivery platforms offer convenience and choice.
2. **Scalable Infrastructure**: Scalable technology infrastructure supports growth and adapts to fluctuating demand. Cloud computing and scalable software solutions provide agility and operational flexibility.
3. **Partnerships and Ecosystems**: Collaborations with tech startups, logistics providers, and e-commerce platforms create synergies and expand service offerings. Ecosystem partnerships enhance operational efficiency and market reach.

Regulatory and Safety Considerations

1. **Regulatory Compliance**: Navigating regulatory frameworks for autonomous vehicles and drone deliveries requires adherence to safety standards and operational guidelines. Collaboration with regulators ensures compliance and promotes industry growth.
2. **Data Privacy and Security**: Protecting customer data and ensuring cybersecurity are paramount. Secure data

management practices safeguard sensitive information and build trust with customers.
3. **Ethical AI Use**: Ethical considerations in AI development and deployment, such as algorithm bias and data privacy, require proactive measures. Businesses must prioritize fairness and accountability in AI applications.

Investing in Talent and Innovation

1. **Skills Development**: Continuous training and upskilling prepare employees for technological advancements. Investing in talent development fosters innovation and enables employees to embrace new technologies confidently.
2. **Innovation Centers and Labs**: Establishing innovation centers and labs encourages experimentation and fosters a culture of innovation. These hubs drive research and development of new technologies and solutions.
3. **Future-Proofing Strategies**: Anticipating future trends and disruptions allows businesses to proactively adapt and innovate. Strategic planning and scenario analysis mitigate risks and capitalize on emerging opportunities.

Conclusion

The future of delivery logistics is shaped by rapid technological advancements, evolving consumer expectations, and sustainability imperatives. By embracing autonomous vehicles, enhancing sustainability practices, prioritizing customer experience, leveraging data analytics, adopting blockchain technology, ensuring regulatory compliance, fostering agility, investing in talent, and fostering innovation, your delivery business can thrive in a dynamic and competitive landscape. In the next chapter, we will explore case studies and success stories of businesses that have successfully implemented innovative delivery solutions, providing valuable insights and inspiration for your own journey.

Conclusion: Embracing Success in Your Delivery Business

Congratulations on completing this journey through the world of delivery business management! Throughout this book, we've explored every facet of starting, growing, and innovating within the delivery industry. From laying the foundational principles to embracing cutting-edge technologies and anticipating future trends, you've gained valuable insights to propel your business forward.

As you embark on implementing these strategies and principles, remember that success in the delivery business is not just about logistics—it's about building relationships, exceeding expectations, and adapting to a rapidly evolving landscape. Here's a final word of encouragement and well-wishes as you chart your course:

Embrace Innovation: Continuously seek new technologies and methodologies that enhance efficiency, reduce costs, and improve customer satisfaction. Innovation is the key to staying competitive and meeting the demands of a modern marketplace.

Focus on Customer Experience: Put your customers at the center of everything you do. By delivering exceptional service, maintaining transparency, and personalizing interactions, you'll cultivate loyal customers who are your best advocates.

Adaptability is Key: The delivery industry is dynamic, influenced by technological advancements, regulatory changes, and shifting consumer preferences. Stay agile and adaptable, ready to pivot and seize opportunities as they arise.

Build a Strong Team: Your team is your greatest asset. Invest in their development, empower them to take initiative, and foster a culture of collaboration and innovation. Together, you can achieve remarkable success.

Sustainability Matters: Embrace sustainable practices that benefit both your business and the environment. From eco-friendly packaging to electric vehicles, contribute positively to the communities you serve.

Celebrate Milestones: Take time to celebrate your achievements, both big and small. Recognize the hard work and dedication that have brought you this far and use these milestones as motivation for future endeavors.

With these principles in mind and armed with the knowledge gained from this book, may your delivery business thrive and grow exponentially. Your dedication to excellence and commitment to delivering value will undoubtedly set you apart in the competitive landscape.

Here's wishing you all the best in your journey towards success in the delivery business. May each delivery bring you closer to your goals, and may your business continue to prosper and make a positive impact in the lives of your customers and communities.

Best wishes for success!

www.ingramcontent.com/pod-product-compliance
Lightning Source LLC
Chambersburg PA
CBHW072051230526
45479CB00010B/679